Second Thoughts
about the Second Coming

Second Thoughts about the Second Coming

Understanding the End Times,
Our Future, and Christian Hope

Ronald J. Allen
Robert D. Cornwall

WESTMINSTER
JOHN KNOX PRESS
LOUISVILLE • KENTUCKY

First edition
Published by Westminster John Knox Press
Louisville, Kentucky

23 24 25 26 27 28 29 30 31 32—10 9 8 7 6 5 4 3 2 1

Unless otherwise indicated, Scripture quotations are from the New Revised Standard Version of the Bible, copyright © 1989 by the Division of Christian Education of the National Council of the Churches of Christ in the U.S.A., and are used by permission. Scripture quotations marked NIV are from *The Holy Bible, New International Version.* Copyright © 1973, 1978, 1984, 2011 by Biblica, Inc.® Used by permission. All rights reserved worldwide.

All citations from the Pseudepigrapha are from James H. Charlesworth, editor, *The Old Testament Pseudepigrapha* (Garden City, NY: Doubleday and Co., 1983), vol. 1.

Book design by Sharon Adams
Cover design by designpointinc.com

Library of Congress Cataloging-in-Publication Data

Names: Allen, Ronald J. (Ronald James), 1949- author. | Cornwall, Robert D., 1958- author.
Title: Second thoughts about the Second Coming : understanding the end times, our future, and Christian hope / Ronald J. Allen, Robert D. Cornwall.
Description: First edition. | Louisville, Kentucky : Westminster John Knox Press, [2023] | Includes bibliographical references. | Summary: "Allen and Cornwall help readers clarify what they believe about the second coming of Jesus and the afterlife, reviewing the many ways these things have been interpreted through history and assisting readers in identifying the viewpoints that they find meaningful"— Provided by publisher.
Identifiers: LCCN 2022054467 (print) | LCCN 2022054468 (ebook) | ISBN 9780664268060 (paperback) | ISBN 9781646983063 (ebook)
Subjects: LCSH: End of the world. | Second Advent.
Classification: LCC BT877 .A45 2023 (print) | LCC BT877 (ebook) | DDC 236/.9—dc23/eng/20230117
LC record available at https://lccn.loc.gov/2022054467
LC ebook record available at https://lccn.loc.gov/2022054468

Most Westminster John Knox Press books are available at special quantity discounts when purchased in bulk by corporations, organizations, and special-interest groups. For more information, please e-mail SpecialSales@wjkbooks.com.

Contents

Acknowledgments

Every book has an origin story, especially one that is jointly authored. This book is no different. While we could go back to years of friendship as the foundation, the book was conceived over a breakfast in the fall of 2019. While Bob was on sabbatical, Ron had come up to Troy, Michigan, to lead a workshop with the church Bob served—Central Woodward Christian Church (Disciples of Christ). Ron suggested that he and Bob write a book together. Bob, knowing that Ron had recently published a commentary on Revelation, suggested they write a book about eschatology (last things). The rest is history.

When it comes to writing a book, it takes something like a village to bring it to fruition. This is where we might thank our agents—but we don't have agents. We are thankful that the folks at Westminster John Knox Press, principally its editor-in-chief, Bob Ratcliff, liked the idea. Then when he shared the idea with the marketing people, they liked it as well. The response was positive, but they wanted us to write a book not for scholars or preachers, but for a general audience. That was our idea as well, but they helped us hone the project so it would meet the needs of the people in churches like the ones where Bob and Ron have taught the Bible over the years. We're grateful for their advice and guidance along the way.

We must thank the congregations where we've preached and taught Bible studies. We appreciate them for their curiosity and for asking good questions that have pushed us to refine our own thinking.

While we are responsible for the content of this book, we would like to thank several people who read all or parts of the book, offering helpful suggestions and constructive criticism. They include Monica Mitri, Martyn Whittock, Steve Kindle, and Ruth Myers Moore. Hermann Weinlick edited the book with precision.

We would like to thank our spouses, Cheryl Cornwall and Linda McKiernan-Allen. They have been understanding of our predilection/need to write. Whether or not they read what we have written over the years, they remain supportive. For that we give thanks.

Finally, as this is a work intended for the church, we thank God for being ever present in our endeavors. May this book be a gift to the church and honor the God we serve in Jesus Christ.

Blessings,
Bob Cornwall and Ron Allen

Preface

The idea for this book began in the real-life experiences of the two authors, Bob and Ron. Ron was a guest leading a Bible study in a local congregation when a participant asked a question that both of us have been asked many times: "What does the Bible really teach about the second coming of Jesus?" Several other participants nodded their heads as if to say, "We have that question too." Ron asked the participant to clarify why the question was important. The response indicated that several participants in the study were friends with members of another congregation that lays great emphasis on the second coming. "Over there, you would think the Bible is not about anything else," commented one of the people in the room. Another added, "They find the second coming everywhere in the Bible—not only in Matthew, Mark, Luke, Paul, the book of Revelation, but also in Daniel, Ezekiel, Isaiah, and those little prophets whose names I cannot pronounce." Someone at the other end of the table observed, "We don't hear much about the second coming in our church." "So," the first questioner picked up, "please tell us what the Bible *really* teaches about the second coming of Jesus."

Bob's experience with the topic of the second coming goes back to his youth. Through music such as Larry Norman's "I Wish We'd All Been Ready," books such as Hal Lindsey's *The Late Great Planet Earth,* and sermons at church, he heard the message that we were living in the last days before Jesus returns, so be prepared, because you don't want to be left behind. As a pastor teaching Bible studies, Bob also discovered deep interest among church members when it comes to questions about the end of the age and life after death. When he asked what biblical books they wanted to study, they asked for Daniel and Revelation. They wanted to know how to read these books responsibly.

Concern about the future persists, as seen in the continued popularity of the *Left Behind* series of books and movies as expressions of contemporary belief that we are living in the last days before Jesus' return. The message of these books and movies, along with others like them, is that we must be ready for Jesus' return or face the consequences. The phenomenal sales of these materials strongly suggest that Christians and the public at large have questions about what the future holds. Likewise, in the early twenty-first century, widespread concern about the environmental crisis, political polarization, economic instability, and continuing violence around the world and at home contribute to a sense of anxiety about the future. For many Christians, belief in the second coming of Jesus offers a sense of hope for a future beyond this life.

Given this environment, Bob and Ron have noticed a curious phenomenon, especially in mainline Protestant churches such as the United Methodist Church, the Presbyterian Church (U.S.A.), the Episcopal Church, the United Church of Christ, the Evangelical Lutheran Church, and the Christian Church (Disciples of Christ). On the one hand, as we have noted, many people in these congregations—and many others—are curious about the second coming, as well as about life after death. They want to know the answer to questions like these: "Will God do something to make things right?" "What happens when I die?" "Will I see my mother and father in heaven?" On the other hand, preachers and teachers seldom directly address such questions.

In this season of uncertainty in the culture and the church, we believe it's important that the church think seriously not only about the second coming but more broadly about what the Christian faith has to say about the future. Therefore, we believe two things need to occur. (1) Christians should identify what people in the Bible and the Christian tradition believed about these things. (2) Christians then need to identify what we believe about the second coming, life after death, and the hope for the future. What Christians believe about what lies ahead will contribute to how we live in the present.

We hope this book helps readers—as individuals and in groups—to achieve greater clarity as to what they believe about the future. We try to describe as clearly as possible a wide range of viewpoints, and when we disagree with a viewpoint, we try to speak respectfully about it. We hope to open windows of understanding that allow readers to gain a better sense of each viewpoint. We seek, as far as possible, to let each perspective speak for itself. Of course, we raise questions and compare and contrast positions, but we try to do so in a conversational spirit that provides readers with information that allows them to come to their own conclusions.

We tackle a set of complicated theological issues in this book. Because it's impossible to completely avoid using technical theological terminology, when we use a technical term the first time—like "eschatology," a term that appears regularly in the book—we provide a definition (often in parentheses). We've also created a glossary for quick reference to important terms. We hope that this book will contribute to a better understanding of an important topic and offer a word of encouragement when it comes to how we perceive the future as Christians.

Introduction

We try not to predict the future in this book, because neither of us knows what the future looks like. However, we do try to explain how the churches have interpreted matters such as the second coming and life after death from the biblical period to the present. We don't try to convince readers to adopt a particular point of view. Instead, we outline major points of view from the past and the present relating to both the second coming of Jesus and life beyond death. In doing so, we seek to help readers think about the strengths and weaknesses of the various viewpoints so that they can make their own decisions about what they believe on such matters.

Oliver Wendell Holmes Sr., the father of the famous justice of the Supreme Court Oliver Wendell Holmes Jr., is reported to have said, "Some people are so heavenly minded that they are no earthly good." To be sure, Christians and others can be distracted by thinking about things to come. But what we believe about the future and its possibilities affects how we live in the present. And how we live in the present affects the kind of future we will have.

The Second Coming Is Part of a Bigger Discussion about God's Ultimate Purposes

In much of Christianity, the phrase "the second coming" refers to Jesus' future return to earth from heaven, accompanied by angels and great cosmic disturbance. This view often envisions violent actions that bring about the defeat of evil. After these things occur, God will establish a renewed world. Many Christians think this is the *only* way to interpret the idea of the second coming. But is this true?

While many emphasize Jesus' second coming when they think about God's future for creation, this is only one aspect of a larger discussion about God's ultimate purposes. The theological term or category that covers this discussion is "eschatology" (pronounced *es-ka-TA-lo-jee*). The word comes from two Greek words: *eschatos* means "last," and *logos* means "thinking about" or "study of." The word "eschatology" refers to the study of what people believe about last things or, more broadly, God's ultimate purposes for humanity and the universe itself. As we shall see in this book, some people believe that God's ultimate purposes will be accomplished within history, while others believe God's purposes will be accomplished beyond history.

The second coming, as we described it above, is part of a particular form of eschatology called apocalyptic eschatology. Readers will recognize that the word "apocalyptic" is closely related to the word "apocalypse," which we often associate with destruction. News reporters might refer to a war zone scarred by burned buildings, blackened trees, and dead bodies as an "apocalyptic scene." However, when it comes to the Bible and Christian reflection, it is too limiting to think of the apocalyptic event only in destructive terms. In Greek, the basic meaning of "apocalyptic" is "to reveal." Some writers in both the ancient and contemporary worlds use the word "apocalyptic" to refer to God revealing God's ultimate purposes through cataclysmic events that bring the present age to an end and inaugurate a new age.

In the early Christian movement, most believers expected the second coming to be a pivotal, apocalyptic event marking the end of the present world and the beginning of a new world. This new era is often called the Realm (Kingdom) of God. In this apocalyptic way of thinking, the old world is characterized by idolatry, animosity, injustice, violence, scarcity, and death, while the Realm of God will be a world of authentic worship, love, justice, peace, abundance, and eternal life. Some first-century believers placed less emphasis on a singular cosmically transforming event and more emphasis on the soul making a journey to heaven. Both groups believed that aspects of the future hope were partially realized in the present.

There are several terms that Christians associate with such eschatology that we use in this book. These terms include "Kingdom (Realm) of God," "last days," "last things," "end times," "great transformation," and "consummation." When we say we have "second thoughts about the second coming," we have in mind not only the event of Jesus' return at the end of the age, but also the larger set of concerns related to the coming of the Realm of God and the fulfillment of God's ultimate purposes (eschatology!). The time has come to think clearly about what we believe about the future, the consequences of those beliefs, and how we should respond to what the future might hold for us.

Three Things to Keep in Mind When Considering the Second Coming

When we consider the second coming, we should keep three things in mind.

First, language about the second coming comes from the world of the Bible, which in many ways is very different from our world today. So we need to pay attention to the differences between the contexts of the ancient world and our own.

Second, we should avoid speaking of *the* biblical perspective or *the* Christian perspective, on the second coming specifically or on God's eschatological purposes more generally. The Bible contains different voices that speak in different ways. Christians need to figure out what to do with such differences.

Third, Christian tradition, as it has developed over the centuries, also offers diverse perspectives on what the future holds for us. We are the heirs of these diverse perspectives, some of which no longer hold true for some people today, while other perspectives continue to speak to how we think on such matters. Even as we consider tradition, we need to bring into the conversation knowledge from the contemporary world. Context matters with respect to how these views have developed and continue to develop.

Putting these things together, we can decide what we *truly* believe about the future. What we believe about the future often goes a long way toward determining the way we live in the present. If we have an optimistic view of the future, we may give ourselves more fully to the present. If we have a negative view of the future, we may step back from taking responsibility for the present.

What You Will Find in the Book

This book is organized chronologically. We follow themes related to the second coming and the afterlife from their initial appearance in Jewish and Christian communities, through their interpretation and reinterpretation in history, until we reach the present.

- In Section One, we focus on God's ultimate purposes in the Old Testament and in the New Testament. We concentrate on Daniel, Paul, the four Gospels, 2 Peter, Jude, and Revelation.
- In Section Two, we trace the two main streams of thought through history beginning in the second century CE. One stream is associated with Eastern Christianity (Greek/Syriac) beginning with Origen and taking us through the aftermath of the fall of the Eastern Roman (Byzantine) Empire in the fifteenth century. We've divided the Western (Latin) stream into two chapters. One chapter takes the reader from the third century CE through the Middle Ages to the eve of the Reformation.

The other chapter begins with the Reformation in the sixteenth century and takes things up to the beginning of the nineteenth century.

- In Section Three, we focus on interpretations of God's ultimate purposes that have emerged over the past two centuries and remain popular to the present moment. These interpretations can be categorized as premillennialism/dispensationalism, postmillennialism, and amillennialism.

- In Section Four, we consider several current perspectives on Christian eschatology. These include realized eschatology, theology of hope, liberation theology, open and relational theologies, and contemporary Orthodox theology.

- While throughout the book we lift up beliefs about the life to come, we bring these ideas and beliefs together in Section Five, so readers can easily compare and contrast them.

- In the appendixes you will find the glossary noted above, which defines key technical theological words and ideas found in this book, as well as a study guide outlining six sessions for small group use.

What Do Bob and Ron Think?

Bob has an eclectic theology and way of thinking about the church. He grew up on the West Coast, where his journey took him through Pentecostal, Baptist, Presbyterian, and Episcopal families. Since seminary, he has been a member of the Christian Church (Disciples of Christ), the denomination in which he was ordained.[1] When it comes to the second coming, he draws from several perspectives, including apocalyptic theology (Jürgen Moltmann), liberation theology, open theism, and Eastern Orthodoxy.

Ron grew up in the Ozark Mountains in southeast Missouri and is a lifelong member of the Christian Church (Disciples of Christ). Because the Disciples do not have formal creeds, they don't have a normative understanding of the second coming. One of their founders, Alexander Campbell, was a postmillennialist. Another founder, Barton Stone, adopted that view after toying with the premillennialism of William Miller early in the nineteenth century (see p. 78). Ron grew up with a historic open-ended approach to the second coming (pp. 91–94). In adulthood, he evolved into a process thinker. Process theology doesn't anticipate a single cosmic event in which Jesus interrupts history to replace the present world with a new one, but believes that God is ever and always present, offering every moment the opportunity to embrace as much love, justice, peace, abundance, and life as that moment affords.

Bob and Ron write with respect for other points of view. In this book, we seek to represent all perspectives fairly. We aim to avoid caricaturing and dismissing others. Indeed, disrespect, associated with caricature, name-calling, and dismissal, works against the values of the fruit of the second coming. We also bring differing professional approaches to this conversation. While both of us are ordained Disciples ministers, Ron trained as a biblical scholar, focusing on the New Testament and preaching. He taught these things for thirty-seven years at Christian Theological Seminary. Bob spent the past two decades as a local pastor but trained as a historical theologian/church historian. The book emerged as a conversation between the two of us; so we take responsibility not only for the parts we gave primary authorship to but for the whole of the book.

Online Resources for Preaching

Although we wrote this book with a general audience in mind, we hope preachers will find the material in the book of interest. So, for preachers, we've developed two online resources to help preachers engage the second coming in the pulpit. One of these resources is *Sermon Series on the Second Coming*, which includes both a general orientation to the subject and suggestions for sermon series based on biblical texts and topics.

The second resource is *Preaching the Second Coming from the Christian Year and the Lectionary*. This guide calls attention to ways in which expectation for the second coming shapes the Year and the lectionary. Preachers may prefer to frame this concern more broadly, as the expectation for the Realm of God or the fulfillment of God's purposes for humankind and nature. In any event, this guide also highlights days and seasons in the Christian Year, as well as texts in the lectionary that provide natural opportunities for thinking with the congregation about how to understand and respond to these texts and themes.

You can find both resources at www.wjkbooks.com/Second Coming.

Sending the Book Forward in Prayer

In this book, we emphasize diverse understandings of eschatology in history and today. Yet, despite the diversity, all Christian forms of thinking about the future known to us presume that God ultimately yearns for conditions of existence (whether in this world or some other world) to align more closely with God's unrelenting desire for love, grace, justice, peace, freedom, and abundance for all. We offer this book out of our love for the church and the wider community. Therefore, we offer it with the prayer that it can help us recognize that God yearns to empower us to join with God in doing our part to bring God's Realm into fruition in this life and/ or the next (depending on your point of view).

SECTION ONE

"I Wish We'd All Been Ready"

Voices from the Bible

The Bible is the most important resource for the Christian community. It serves, for most Christians, as a normative authority for matters of doctrine and practice. While Christians see the nature of this authority in diverse ways, many Christians recognize that different biblical voices speak differently about many distinct subjects. This diversity includes views of the second coming of Jesus and the afterlife.

In the two chapters that make up this section, we survey the main biblical voices regarding the second coming and the afterlife. We explore the several ways the biblical writers speak about God's ultimate purposes for the world and especially for humanity. We start in chapter 1 with voices in the Old Testament. While the first thirty-nine books do not directly mention the second coming, they provide valuable background. Then, in chapter 2, we turn to the New Testament voices that emphasize the second coming, especially the first three Gospels and Acts, the letters of Paul, 2 Peter, and Jude, and the book of Revelation. We close by looking at the Gospel and Letters of John, which put less emphasis on the apocalyptic return of Jesus and more emphasis on the realization of God's purposes in the present, as well as the individual's journey to heaven and eternal communion with God. In such a short study we cannot consider every text that mentions the second coming and the afterlife, but we can consider representative voices.

We join biblical scholars and theologians who seek to interpret the Bible in light of what the biblical writers intended to say to their communities in their historical settings. Many biblical writers anticipated future events. However, they typically expected things would happen soon, not hundreds of years in the future. Therefore, we write this part of the book with the assumption that the biblical authors were *not* predicting events that would take place centuries later, including the twenty-first century.

While we believe the biblical writers didn't see themselves predicting events far into the future, as the book unfolds we'll meet Christians who see things differently. For some interpreters, the Bible speaks about events happening now, leading them to see signs that the apocalyptic second coming of Jesus is imminent. Many Christians understand this to be *the* biblical perspective. Before we get to these later interpretations, in the following two chapters we explore how the biblical authors imagined God's ultimate purposes, including the second coming and life after death.

1

The Old Testament

The Old Testament doesn't directly refer to the second coming. Most Old Testament voices assume that God's ultimate purposes will be fulfilled within the present historical context. As we'll see, there is a stream of thought within these traditions that envisions an existence beyond the grave. However, these traditions don't completely correspond with what Christians mean by heaven and hell. At the same time, the apocalyptic literature that emerged after Israel returned from the exile provided the foundation for the idea of Jesus' second coming.

God Seeks to Fulfill the Divine Purposes in This World

Many of the Old Testament voices agree on three things. (1) God created the world as a good place, with everything fitting together in mutually supportive relationships (Gen. 1:1–2:4). Everything should work together for the good of all, which is a state of blessing. (2) The human family violated God's purposes, diminishing the quality of life for all, which led to violence, the disruption of creation, and death (Gen. 3–4). (3) God offered the human family a way to repair the damage by making a covenant with Israel.

In so doing, God called Israel to live in such a way that other communities might join them in enjoying God's original blessing. In the words of Second Isaiah, God chose Israel to be "a light to the nations." That is, Second Isaiah envisioned Israel modeling how all human families could live in a relationship with God and one another in a context of blessing (Isa. 42:6–7). This assumes that God intends human communities to live together in a covenant relationship that leads to blessing for all in the present world. Only much later does Jewish tradition begin to speak of God bringing the present world to a close and inaugurating a new one.

God's blessings, as expressed in the Old Testament, may involve both inner experience and physical existence. In the book of Deuteronomy, Moses tells Israel, as they are about to enter the promised land, that God will provide them with everything they need for a secure and sustainable life. This includes the assurance that God loves them, together with the promise that the ground will be fruitful, the rain will fall, and more. God also will turn away illness and disease. In addition, their neighbors won't overrun them, so they can safely dwell in the land (e.g., Deut. 7:12–16; 28:1–14). The covenant contains provisions so that everyone in the community—including widow, orphan, and stranger—will have the resources necessary for life (e.g., Deut. 10:18–19; 14:29). God intends for Israel to have a rich and full experience in a land "flowing with milk and honey" (e.g., Exod. 3:8; Deut. 6:3).

God graciously made a covenant with Israel that came with certain instructions or stipulations. Sometimes called laws, they guide the people in living the way of blessing. The Ten Commandments are the most familiar of the guidelines (Deut. 5:6–21; cf. Exod. 20:2–17), but Exodus, Leviticus, and Deuteronomy contain many more guidelines. Accordingly, when the community obeys the commandments, blessing follows; when the community disobeys, the people are cursed (e.g., Deut. 11:26–28; 27:11–29:1). The conditions of the curse are opposite those of blessing: tensions with God, tensions with others in the community, tensions between the community and other communities, exploitation, injustice, violence, and disruption in the community's relationship with nature. As with the circumstances of blessing, the curse takes place within this world.

When the community is disobedient, God offers repentance as a way of moving from being cursed to being blessed. Repentance means turning away from disobedience toward obedience. If the community doesn't repent, God will curse it. To be sure, not all biblical writers affirm this perspective. The book of Job, for instance, suggests that sometimes obedient people experience a cursed life while the disobedient appear to prosper. Indeed, throughout history, people have questioned the idea that obedience leads to blessing and disobedience results in curses. Nevertheless, that view is present in the Bible.

The prophets generally assume the mind-set of obedience, disobedience, and repentance. When the community is disobedient, the prophets call attention to the violations of the covenant. The prophets may invite the people to repent, cease the violation, and return to the covenantal values and practices that bring blessing. Disobedience often involves idolatry, injustice, exploitation, and violence. It can also involve a lack of trust in the promises and power of God. In the case of idolatry, injustice, exploitation, and violence, the prophet may urge the community to repent of idolatry and other acts of disobedience and return to authentic worship and covenantal living. For example, Ezekiel admonishes the community, "Repent and turn away from your idols" (Ezek. 14:6). In Ezekiel, the prophet urges the community in seasons of uncertainty to continue to trust that God will keep God's promises. During the Babylonian exile, Second Isaiah urges the community to once again have confidence that God is more powerful than the Babylonian deities and will free the community from captivity (Isa. 44:22; 45:22).

The prophets sometimes refer to "the Day of the Lord," a time when God will act decisively. God's actions on that day depend upon circumstances. It could be a day of judgment on those who were disobedient, in Israel as well as in other nations. It could refer to God acting to redeem Israel or others. Thus, "the Day of the Lord" can include both punishment and redemption.

These actions are understood to take place within Israel's historical existence (Isa. 2:12; Amos 5:18–20; Zeph. 1:8; Mal. 4:2). Although the language "the Day of the Lord" is sometimes later associated with the second coming of Jesus, the Old Testament doesn't have Jesus in view.

The Writings or Wisdom literature envision God's purposes being fulfilled in terms of present quality of life. This literature—Proverbs, Job, Ecclesiastes, the Song of Songs, and many psalms—makes less use of covenant language. It tends to contrast a life of wisdom with a life of foolishness (folly). According to this tradition, God has arranged the world in an orderly way so that the common good of all can be achieved (e.g., Prov. 3:19–20). Humans discover this order by paying attention to their experiences in the world. These experiences are then formulated into sayings (such as proverbs) that teach people how to live in this world. For example, Proverbs points to the ants who, without a leader, work industriously all summer to prepare food for the winter (Prov. 6:6–8). The wise life is prosperous, abundant, and marked by a life of blessing.

Foolishness results from ignoring God's wisdom. Foolish people or communities usually live in a way that benefits themselves without any concern for how their behavior affects others. For example, when scoundrels manifest deceptive behavior, fooling others and "sowing discord," they bring "damage beyond repair" on themselves (Prov. 6:12–15). Both wisdom and folly take place within contemporary life.

Moving toward an End-Time Hope

In 597 BCE, after the Babylonians invaded Judah, captured Jerusalem, laid waste the land, and destroyed the temple, the leaders of Judah were exiled to Babylon. Psalm 137:1 captures the feeling of this event: "There we sat down and there we wept when we remembered Zion [Jerusalem]." The exile was the setting in which ideas began to take shape that led to the idea of the second coming of Jesus.

We stress the exilic setting because some Christians (and many others) claim that the end-time framework serves as an escape from dealing with the complications of life and even as an excuse for avoiding responsibility for life in this world. "We'll just wait for God to fix things." In some respects, the opposite is true. End-time thinking is born in the teeth of struggle. It offers a way to make sense of disappointment and difficulty. It offers hope that can inspire the community to continue being faithful during the long season of struggle.

The exile raised penetrating questions for the community. What caused the exile? Why did it happen? What do we do now? How does our distinctive culture relate to the alien Babylonian culture? What can we believe will happen to us in the future? What will God do, especially in comparison to the Babylonian gods? What is our mission? These questions continued after the exiles returned from Babylon because their postexilic life took place as a colony of Persia. Although the Persians were more friendly than the Babylonians, the Jewish community was still beholden to an outside nation. Judah was subsequently occupied by a series of other nations (except for a brief period) through the end of the Roman Empire.

We can trace the emergence of end-time thinking by looking at representative texts in Isaiah, Zechariah, and Daniel. Isaiah 40–55 was written during the exile and highlights the idea that God will do a new thing by freeing the exiles from captivity and leading them back through the wilderness to Judah (e.g., Isa. 43:19). Isaiah 56–66, often called Third Isaiah, was written after the return from exile, when Persia ruled. The community was experiencing painful internal conflict, and Judah's infrastructure was in disrepair. Speaking to this disheartened community, Isaiah pleads for God to "tear open the heavens and come down" (Isa. 64:1). In a style that gets amplified in the New Testament, Isaiah has God say: "I am about to create new heavens and a new earth" (Isa. 65:17). To be sure, this "new earth" will be a continuation of the present earth, but as Isaiah 65:18–25 exults, the structures of life on the earth will be radically transformed to the point that "the wolf and the lamb shall feed together" and "they shall not hurt or destroy on all my holy mountain" (Isa. 65:25).

Zechariah 9–14 adds wrinkles to this vision that become part of later end-time thinking. On the Day of the Lord, a great battle will take place between the forces of God and their enemies (Zech. 14:1–5). God will come with the holy ones to resolve conflict and establish God's rule over all peoples. God will transform the created order so that cold and frost no longer exist, daylight lasts twenty-four hours (there will be no night), and the land around Jerusalem will be fertile. Moreover, the division between Jews and Gentiles will disappear when Judah's former enemies come to Jerusalem to worship God (Zech. 14:5–19).

Daniel 7–12: Window into End-Time Thinking

Whereas Isaiah and Zechariah contain hints about end-time thinking, Daniel 7–12 is the only part of the Old Testament exhibiting a fully developed end-time perspective. As we point out earlier, the book of Daniel isn't the only piece of Jewish literature with an apocalyptic flavor from 300 BCE to 200 CE. Some of this extrabiblical literature predates Daniel. For example, parts of *1 Enoch* may date to the third century BCE. Similar Jewish books include *4 Ezra*, *2 Baruch*, and *The Testaments of the Twelve Patriarchs*.[1]

Daniel 7–12 was written during 168–165 BCE, when the Greeks occupied the Holy Land and prohibited the Jews from many of their distinctive religious practices. The Greeks actively persecuted Jews, killing many of them, and set up a shrine to Zeus in the temple. This led to an armed revolt led by Judas Maccabeus and his family.

Daniel uses word pictures many people today find confusing because the pictures seem surreal. For instance, Daniel pictures a beast with iron teeth, bronze claws, ten horns on its head, along with one horn that has eyes and a mouth that speaks arrogantly (Dan. 7:19–20). While we might find the language odd, it was a commonplace way for apocalyptic writers to speak of specific individuals, communities, and events. Daniel uses the image of the beast to describe the arrogant Greek ruler whose actions and behaviors prompted the Jewish revolt. Daniel uses these word pictures to interpret current and present events as well as pointing toward God's activity in the present and future. It's important to remember that the future pictured by Daniel and other apocalyptic writings of the period envisions events taking place within Daniel's own time or that might take place in the foreseeable future.

Other elements in Daniel that appear in later apocalyptic visions include notions of an intense period of suffering immediately before the end ("a time of anguish"), a book in which the names of the saved are found, and the idea that God has predetermined what the future holds. God hid these things as a "mystery" until they're revealed near the end of days (Dan. 12:1–3).

Daniel 7:9–14 speaks of God sending to earth "one like a human being" ("one like a son of man")—a figure in God's heavenly court—to destroy forces hostile to God and establish God's rule in a remade world. The prophet seeks to reassure the community that God will deliver them, while discouraging them from joining the revolt, because God will take care of things for them. This reveals one of the classic purposes of end-time writings: to encourage faithfulness in the face of oppression and suffering. When necessary, these authors exhort the community to repent of complacency and continued embrace of the practices and values of the old age.

In Daniel 12:1–3, the prophet offers a picture of the new life by revealing a final judgment. The dead will awaken either to shame and everlasting contempt (eternal punishment) or to everlasting life. Until the final judgment, the dead are simply dead, as if asleep. As part of this first unmistakable reference to resurrection in the Bible, Daniel describes the resurrected faithful shining "like the brightness of the sky . . . like the stars forever." In the new world, the righteous will have new bodies not subject to decay.

For Daniel, God has the final power over history and has already determined when the end will come. The moment of the great transformation doesn't depend on human effort, because God will bring it about. Sometimes God works through social processes, but eventually God and the angels will intervene in history. The heavenly retinue dismantles the structures of the old world and replaces them with the values and practices of the new world.

While human beings won't bring about this new world through their own efforts, they should not wait passively for the new age. Human beings—as individuals and as communities—can bear witness to the coming transformation by living faithfully according to God's purposes. They also can invite others to repent of their complicity with the values, rulers, and practices of the old age and live according to the values of the new age. Accordingly, individuals and communities need to prepare for the final judgment and the separation between those experiencing everlasting punishment and everlasting life.

The new world—also known as the Realm of God, new creation, new age, and age to come—will have many of the qualities of blessing we spoke of earlier, but with a decisive difference. The new age will be everlasting, with people living in resurrection bodies. Whereas the prophets envisioned the repair of present conditions, apocalyptic writers believe the present world is in such disrepair that God needs to replace it.

Resurrection and Praying for the Dead in 2 Maccabees

The books of 1 and 2 Maccabees, which show up in many Bibles in the section titled The Apocrypha, offer slightly different interpretations of similar stories. Second Maccabees was likely written between 125 and 63 BCE and portrays many Jewish people abandoning Judaism for non-Jewish ways. The author of 2 Maccabees wanted to encourage the Jewish community to renounce compromise with non-Jewish ways of living and adhere to Jewish values and practices. The author seeks to accomplish this by retelling many of the stories found in 1 Maccabees, thereby offering the heroes and heroines of 1 Maccabees as models of faithfulness in suffering martyrdom rather than compromise with an alien culture. The faithful suffer and die in the confidence God will raise them from the dead (e.g., 2 Macc. 7:14, 23).

In 2 Maccabees 12:39–45, Judas Maccabeus, the leader of the Maccabeans, seeks to recover the bodies of Jewish people who died during the time of oppression. As he does so, he discovers "sacred tokens" representing pagan deities hidden on the bodies. The dead had portrayed themselves as being faithful, even as they embraced Greek culture. Therefore, the faithful who were with Judas began to pray that God would blot out the sins of those who died (2 Macc. 12:42). Judas collected a sin offering. "In doing this, [Judas] acted very well and honorably, taking account of the resurrection. For if [Judas] were not expecting that those who had fallen would rise again, it would have been superfluous and foolish to pray for the dead" (2 Macc. 12:43–44).

Some Christians, notably Roman Catholics, look to this passage as the basis for praying for the dead and the doctrine of purgatory. Those who pray in this way believe that at death the soul goes into an interim state where their unforgiven sins are purged. By praying for the dead, believers seek to move those in purgatory toward heaven so they can await the second coming. While we discuss this further in chapter 17 (cf. p. 69), we note now that 2 Maccabees does not explicitly refer to purgatory. Moreover, the New Testament doesn't speak of prayers for the dead, though Paul speaks of people being baptized for the dead (1 Cor. 15:29). There are references to the resurrected Jesus descending "into the lower parts of the earth" (Eph. 4:9–10) and preaching to the spirits in prison (1 Pet. 3:19–20), but the exact meaning of such passages is debated. None of these passages seem to point to a fully developed doctrine of purgatory as we know it today.

2

The New Testament

Jewish apocalyptic thinking provides the framework for understanding most New Testament passages that speak to the second coming of Jesus. Most New Testament books assume that during his earthly ministry Jesus announced the coming of the Realm of God and revealed its presence through his actions. Then, after the resurrection, Jesus ascended to heaven until he returns to earth for the final revealing of the Realm of God. Thus, Jesus didn't reject Judaism but followed the vision revealed in the book of Daniel and similar apocalyptic literature, applying that way of thinking to his own time. Jesus' followers continued that interpretation.

We see this emphasis on cosmic renewal in the ways New Testament writers speak of the Realm of God. In antiquity, a "realm" involved time, place, and activity. The Realm of God is that time when the rule of God shapes all persons, relationships, and places. The Gospels explicitly portray Jesus announcing the purpose of his ministry as manifesting the Realm of God (Mark 1:14–15; Matt. 4:17; Luke 4:16–21). This holistic notion is captured in the phrase "new heaven and new earth" (2 Pet. 3:13; Rev. 21:1). Paul speaks of the new reality as a "new creation" (2 Cor. 5:17). The well-known scholar N. T. Wright points out that the future hope is for God to renew the entire universe.[1] The idea is that God will shape the material world and everything that happens within it according to God's restorative purposes. The future hope is thus not an escape from the world but is God remaking the world so that all live in fullness of blessing.

So, what differentiates the end-time thinking of those who remained committed only to Judaism and the thinking of those who identified with the Jesus movement? Since Jesus was Jewish and the Jesus movement was originally a Jewish movement, one would assume there would be many similarities, especially since many early Jesus followers remained actively Jewish. There are three principal differences. The first difference has to do with agency. For the Jesus movement, Jesus is the final agent through whom God brings about the new age. The second difference concerns the timeline, with the new Jesus movement believing that the end of the age was about to dawn. Thirdly, when it came to the nature of the ministries of Jesus and the early church, they not only announced the coming of the Realm of God (and invited people to repent), but they also embodied the qualities of the coming Realm in their lives.

Jewish views of life after death continued as they did before the Jesus movement emerged. Some of Jesus' followers embraced the Jewish apocalyptic idea that at death the person's mind essentially goes to sleep as the body decays in the earth. On the last day, they believed, God would resurrect the body in a transformed form. Other followers of Jesus sided with Jewish thinkers who adapted the popular Greek idea that human beings are made up of a non-material soul and a physical body. At death, they believed, the immortal soul would leave the body and move to the next world. Some New Testament writers used language associated with both the resurrection of the dead and the immortal soul.

Paul

Paul became a believer in Jesus about 33–35 CE and lived until the mid-60s CE, which means his ministry took place in the first generation of the Jesus movement. He believed that Jesus' death and resurrection was the historical turning point when the old age gave way to the new. He believed the regeneration of the world that began with Jesus' first advent would be completed when Jesus returned for a second advent. In the meantime, the church is called upon to announce this good news and embody the new creation in its actions, attitudes, and relationships. Therefore, the church is a community that represents the new creation in the midst of the old. However, from Paul's standpoint, the churches to whom he wrote did not fully live out the values of the new creation but continued to manifest traits of the old creation. The apostle responds to what he perceives as misrepresentations of the Realm of God that were spreading through the churches. Paul guides the churches on how to better embody the qualities of the Realm of God.

Paul's letters are loaded with apocalyptic language as he addresses the imminent return of Jesus. We illustrate this phenomenon by referring to three of his letters: 1 Thessalonians, 1 Corinthians, and Romans. In each case, the apostle calls attention to particular aspects of the second coming as they relate to the situation of the particular congregation.

Paul wrote 1 Thessalonians between 49 and 51 CE, making it not only the earliest of Paul's letters but also the earliest document in the New Testament. The Thessalonians had expected Jesus to return long before Paul wrote his letter. As time passed and some of the believers died before Jesus returned, some in the community worried that those who died might miss out on God's Realm because they died before Jesus returned. Paul addresses this concern by pointing them to the "day of the Lord" (1 Thess. 5:2). He tells them that the second coming will begin with the cry of the archangel and the sound of a trumpet. Then Jesus will descend from heaven, at which time the dead will rise, along with the faithful who are alive, and together they will meet Jesus in the air so they might live with Jesus forever (1 Thess. 4:13–18).

Some Christians interpret the reference to the faithful being "caught up in the air" as the foundation for the doctrine of the "rapture." However, a careful reading of 1 Thessalonians 4:13–18 doesn't support this idea, since the passage does not refer to a tribulation from which believers will be spared. In 1 Thessalonians, the reference to believers rising into the air suggests how the faithful will experience Jesus' return in glory. Paul acknowledges their concern but then encourages them to embody their future hope in the way they live in the present (1 Thess. 5:1–10).

The congregation at Corinth was dysfunctional. They fought over numerous issues, and in doing so they exhibited behaviors rooted in the old age, with many living as if there would be no final judgment or age to come. In other words, they lived as if there were no eternal consequences to their actions, thereby losing their opportunity to be part of the Realm. Consequently, Paul urges them to reform their attitudes and behavior so they can avoid final condemnation and live forever in a resurrection body.

In his first letter to the Corinthian church, Paul urges the members to live in accord with the attitudes and behaviors of the coming Realm of God, since "the present form of this world is passing away" (1 Cor. 7:31). Paul brings this letter to a culmination with an extended discussion of the second coming and life in a resurrected body in the new age (1 Cor. 15:1–58). Paul begins by establishing the trustworthiness of the claim that God raised Jesus from the dead (1 Cor. 15:1–11). The resurrection of Christ is the "first fruit" of the resurrection of all who have died in faith (15:20, 23). The apostle outlines the sequence of events at the second coming: Christ will raise the dead who belong to him; Christ will destroy the rulers, authorities, powers, and structures that represent the old age; Christ will then destroy death, which is the most potent enemy; Christ will put all things explicitly under his rulership; then Christ will submit himself to the rule of God and hand over the Realm to God (1 Cor. 15:20–28).

Paul pushes language to the limits as he describes the resurrection body. This new body will be as different from the present body as the seed is from the mature plant. There is continuity, but the new body will be unimaginably better than the old

(1 Cor. 15:35–49). As Paul puts it: "flesh and blood" (the body in its present state) "cannot inherit the [Realm] of God." When the last trumpet sounds, God will change the old body into the new "in the twinkling of an eye." While the person continues from old to new, the new body is "imperishable and immortal" (1 Cor. 15:50–57).

Romans is the last of Paul's letters (written in the early 60s). As with the previous letters, Paul wrote to encourage members of the congregation to live according to the values of the new creation rather than the old. We see Paul's end-time framework with particular clarity in Romans 8:19–23:

> For the creation waits with eager longing for the revealing of the children of God. . . . [T]he creation itself will be set free from its bondage to decay and will obtain the freedom of the glory of the children of God. . . . [T]he whole creation has been groaning in labor pains until now; and not only the creation, but we ourselves, who have the first fruits of the Spirit, groan inwardly while we wait for adoption, the redemption of our bodies.

Paul interprets the present situation of the world as "groaning in labor pains." That is, the world awaits the second coming in the way an expectant mother experiences painful contractions. The world's groaning is the intense suffering apocalyptic writers expected as history grows closer to the apocalypse. So, the world awaits release from its suffering, just as a mother longs for release from her birth pangs. But the birth itself—the apocalypse—will result in overflowing joy.

Mark, Matthew, Luke

Mark, Matthew, and Luke (also known as the Synoptic Gospels) wrote during a chaotic period of history. Mark's Gospel likely appeared after the end of the Roman war on the Jewish people and the destruction of the temple in Jerusalem (66–70 CE). Matthew and Luke appeared around a decade later. The fall of

Jerusalem created a crisis in Judaism similar to the crisis triggered by the exile in the sixth century BCE. Jewish communities responded by asking why this happened and what their future would be like. Not only were there tensions between Rome and the Jewish people, but the Jews were of different minds as to how to respond.

Each Gospel writer offered their interpretation of these events. They each saw the second coming serving as God's ultimate response to the savagery the Roman Empire visited upon the Jewish people and the temple, the primary symbol of Judaism. God condemns those who are complicit with the old age. Beyond the final judgment, God will return Jesus to bring about the final and full manifestation of the Realm. While the Gospels share this common core perspective on the second coming, the first three Gospels manifest nuances of difference. Each Gospel writer shaped the story of Jesus to speak to concerns in their particular historical context.

All three Gospels portray John the Baptist as an end-time prophet who announces the coming final judgment (beyond which lies the new world). John calls people to repent (Mark 1:2–8; Matt. 3:1–12; Luke 3:1–20). He speaks in the future tense of the great day of judgment that lies ahead. When the Gospel writers describe the baptism of Jesus by John, they do so in apocalyptic terms (Mark 1:9–11; Matt. 3:13–17; Luke 3:21–22).

The first words that Jesus speaks in each Gospel point to the end-time goal of his ministry. "The time is fulfilled and the [Realm] of God is at hand. Repent, and believe in the good news" (Mark 1:15; cf. Matt 4:17; Luke 4:16–20). As we point out above, the meaning of the expression "the Realm of God" is quite similar here to its meaning in our discussion of Daniel 7–12; namely, it refers to the coming new world in which God ordains qualities of blessing for all who repent.

According to the Synoptic Gospels, Jesus is the final end-time prophet who announces the beginning of the events that lead to the transition from the present world to the beginning of a new world. As such, Jesus calls for listeners to repent (Mark 1:14–15;

Matt. 4:17; Luke 5:32). With both John and Jesus being end-time prophets, their messages are strikingly similar: the Realm of God is coming, so it's time to repent. The main differences have to do with timing and agency. While John sees the Realm being a future event, Jesus envisions it partially beginning in the present. Additionally, Jesus not only proclaims the Realm, but he also serves as God's agent, bringing the Realm into existence.

Apocalyptic references can be found throughout the Gospels, but each writer offers a specific discourse focusing on the second coming as the culmination of God's redeeming work (Mark 13:1–37; Matt. 24:1–44, Luke 21:1–38). Mark's discourse in Mark 13:1–37 can represent what we find in Matthew and Luke. Although Mark's Jesus speaks of future events, Mark sought to interpret current events while also pointing to other imminent events.[2]

As Mark 13 begins, Jesus speaks about the destruction of the temple and the social chaos occurring in 70 CE (such as the "wars and rumors of wars"). These events are signs that the second coming will occur soon. These events are part of the "birth pangs" (Mark 13:1–8). Mark considers the Roman destruction of the temple to be the definitive sign that the end times have begun (Mark 13:14). The final days will be a period of intense suffering "such as has not been since the beginning of the creation" (Mark 13:19). Mark then comes to the main point:

> But in those days, after that suffering, the sun will be darkened, and the moon will not give its light, and the stars will be falling from heaven, and the powers in the heavens will be shaken. Then they will see [the one like a human being, the end-time agent of God] coming in clouds with great power and glory. Then he will send out the angels, and gather [the] elect from the four winds, from the ends of the earth to the ends of heaven. (Mark 13:24–27)

On the one hand, Mark anticipates that this cosmic event will occur within his own generation (Mark 13:30; cf. Mark 9:1). On the other hand, the Markan Jesus advises the community not to be preoccupied with trying to calculate the timing of the second coming. "About that day or hour no one knows, neither the angels in heaven, nor [Jesus], but only [God]" (Mark 13:32). The congregation needs to endure (Mark 13:13). Furthermore, they should "keep alert" (Mark 13:33), which means to continue to live as a community of witnesses to the Realm.

While Mark is electric with the sense that the second coming is at hand, Matthew and Luke anticipate a delay in the return of Jesus. Many in Matthew's community were losing confidence in the second coming and were no longer witnessing with zeal. Matthew seeks to reawaken confidence in the second coming and the importance of making a witness. We see this concern present in a series of four parables found in Matthew 24:45–25:46. Each parable seeks to motivate faithfulness by reminding us that God condemns the unfaithful by consigning them to punishment. Thus, Jesus declares: "Cut [the unfaithful servant] in pieces and put [that servant] with the hypocrites, where there will be weeping and gnashing of teeth" (Matt. 24:51). At the same time, each parable encourages the community as it awaits the second coming to serve faithfully (Matt. 24:45–51), have an adequate supply of oil to keep the lamps lit (Matt. 25:1–13), multiply their witness (Matt. 25:14–30), and share the values of the Realm with those who haven't experienced the Realm (Matt. 25:31–46). Matthew closes with Jesus commissioning his followers to "go" and make disciples through baptism and teaching (Matt. 28:16–20).

We take the Gospel of Luke and the book of Acts together because they have the same author (Luke) and tell one story. Luke–Acts assumes the second coming will bring the old age to a close and launch the new (e.g., Luke 21:25–28; Acts 2:17–21; 3:17–26). It foresees an even longer delay in the return of Jesus than Matthew. Luke–Acts deals with this delay in two ways. First, it gives heightened attention to the Holy Spirit, as seen in the story of the outpouring of the Spirit on the Day of Pentecost (Acts 2:1–42). For Luke, the Holy Spirit is the power of the Realm that is already operating in the church and the world.

Second, Luke tells how the church developed as a missional community that witnesses to Christ until his return. This community is a colony of the new creation within the old. As such, God has called it to invite Gentiles to repent and join the church as it moves toward the Realm of God. For Luke, because of the long delay before the Realm of God breaks into the world, the church must engage in mission. The Holy Spirit makes this possible.

In the book of Acts, Luke offers the reader an interpretive history of the church that emphasizes the church's conflicts (a) with other Jewish communities, (b) with the Roman government, and (c) within the church itself. Luke writes to assure the community that the Spirit empowers the church's witness as it moves providentially toward Christ's return.

The Book of Revelation

Many Christians consider the book of Revelation to be the most dramatic statement about the second coming in the New Testament. Some believe Revelation predicts events taking place today. However, when the book of Revelation speaks of the second coming, it addresses life in the Roman Empire at the end of the first century CE. The imagery in the book of Revelation may seem strange and even frightening to many modern Christians. Some of the imagery, such as God throwing Satan into a lake of fire, can be troubling. So, why bother with the book? Since there are so many questions surrounding the meaning of the book, we'll try to clarify the message of the Revelation by setting it in its historical context.

Ancient readers would have more easily understood the book of Revelation, because it fell in line with other apocalyptic literature such as Daniel and *1 Enoch*. The author—a prophet named John—uses word pictures to refer to people, groups, values, and behaviors present in the Roman Empire around 90 to 95 CE. The empire was a rigid, hierarchical society with Caesar at the top and the elite members of society owning most of the land

and resources and wielding most of the power. The Roman military enforced the so-called "peace of Rome" through the threat of violence. Much of the population lived in poverty and squalor. Besides this, John was concerned about the Roman imperial cult housed in shrines where people paid tribute to Caesar (Rev. 13:11–18). Many of the emperors (Caesars) were divinized after they died, while some in the empire hailed Domitian, the emperor at the time John wrote, as divine during his lifetime. Since Rome's values and practices opposed those of God's Realm, John was concerned that the churches had accommodated themselves too closely with Roman culture, putting them in danger of being condemned at the second coming.

The message of the book of Revelation has both present and future dimensions. John uses word pictures to help the community interpret things happening in its immediate world while pointing toward things yet to occur. Like most apocalyptic writers, John assumes that God controls events in history. Indeed, John's first word-picture reveals that God established Christ as the cosmic ruler through whom God exercises power (Rev. 1:12–16). Christ will return to complete the work of redemption (e.g., Rev. 1:4–8; 22:6–7). The churches can witness with boldness because God has revealed that Christ is already sovereign in heaven over all powers on earth, including Caesar.

John uses literary imagery to reveal that the Roman Empire is nothing less than an instrument of Satan (e.g., Rev. 12:18; 13:1–10; 17:1–18). When believers accommodate the idolatry, injustice, exploitation, and violence of the empire, they cooperate with Satan. John reminds listeners that on the coming day of judgment God will welcome those who endured faithfully into "a new heaven and a new earth" (Rev. 21:1). As for Satan and his followers, they will be cast into a lake of fire (Rev. 20:1–14). Therefore, the community should repent (e.g., Rev. 2:5, 16, 21, 22; 3:3, 19: 9:20–21; 16:11).

John doesn't provide a timeline as to when these things will take place, but he believes they will occur "soon" (e.g., Rev. 1:1; 22:12, 20). While John anticipates a final, cosmic transformation, he believes that the idolatry and injustice present in the empire are already setting the stage for its collapse (Rev. 18:1–24). John wants the reader to contrast Rome's fate with the future in the New Jerusalem.

John uses architectural imagery to describe the new heaven and the new earth (Rev. 21:9–22:5), but he doesn't speak in literal terms of high walls and golden streets. He uses symbolic language to speak of what life will be like after the great transformation. It will be a life of security, beauty, and openness. Through repentance, the community can experience this future life in the present, even when they live in conflict with the empire.

Jude and 2 Peter

Jude and 2 Peter date from the end of the first century or early in the second, making them among the last books of the New Testament to be written. These letters reveal that fervent end-time expectations persisted despite the delay in Jesus' return. Both of these letters address the presence of false teachers who have persuaded some members of their congregations to adopt unfaithful beliefs and immoral behavior.

According to Jude, which may predate 2 Peter, the false teachers and those who follow them will be condemned on the last day (Jude 5–16). Jude quotes the book of *1 Enoch* in support of his argument (Jude 14–15). As we've already noted, the book of *1 Enoch* is a Jewish apocalypse that teaches that the coming end of the age will include a final judgment.

In language strikingly reminiscent of Jude, 2 Peter criticizes false teachers and those who follow them, declaring that they can expect the condemnation "being kept until the day of judgment and destruction of the godless" (2 Pet. 3:7, 10, 11–13). Some in the congregation ask, "Where is the promise of [Jesus'] coming?" In response, 2 Peter uses an argument still used today: "With [God], one day is like a thousand years.... [God] is not slow about [God's] promise, as some think of slowness, but is patient with you, not wanting any to perish, but all to come to repentance" (2 Pet. 3:8–9).

The Gospel and Letters of John

The Gospel and Letters of John agree with other biblical authors that something is wrong with the world and that God will fix things. However, John interpreted things differently, as his perspective on both the present and the future is rooted in a mixture of Jewish philosophy and a modified Platonism similar to the views of the Jewish philosopher Philo.[3] If we understand John's worldview, we can better understand why the Gospel of John places less emphasis on the second coming and more emphasis on the way God's presence is revealed in the present through Jesus. John's view is often called "realized eschatology," in that he focuses on how God's Realm is being revealed in the present.

While Paul, the Synoptic Gospels, and the book of Revelation envision two ages (the present evil age and the coming Realm of God), John envisions two spheres of existence, represented as heaven (above) and the world (below). John's two spheres take place at the same time, although some of the qualities of the world above (heaven) manifest themselves in the world below. Sometimes this dualism is understood to be a contrast between the physical (earthly) and the spiritual (heavenly) realms. The Gospel of John presupposes a beginning (John 1:1–5) and anticipates an end (e.g., John 6:39–40, 54; 12:25, 48), but for the time being the upper and lower spheres of existence move in parallel (and occasionally intersecting) relationship.

We could think of John's two spheres of existence as the upper and lower stories of a two-story house, with heaven above and the world below. However, these are more spheres of experience than distinct spaces. So, while the heavenly sphere is shaped by the immediate, unmediated presence of God, the experience of the world often violates the purposes of God. We can see the main characteristics of these opposing spheres of experience below:

Heaven	World
Life	Death
Love	Hate
Truth	Falsehood
Sight	Blindness
Fullness	Hunger
Freedom	Slavery
Oneness (community)	Division
Belief	Unbelief
Salvation	Condemnation
Born of God	Born of human will
Salvation	Condemnation
Recognizes Jesus as revealer	Does not recognize Jesus as revealer

When John uses the word "world," he generally doesn't have in mind the created order depicted in Genesis 1 and 2. Rather, "world" refers to a negative sphere of existence. Because the world's inhabitants lack adequate awareness of God, they live as if locked in a basement without windows. Therefore, when it comes to the world, they assume that they're experiencing the highest possible existence available to human beings.

According to the Gospel of John, Jesus is the Word (Greek: *logos*), who is with God and who became flesh and dwelt within the world, bringing the qualities of heaven to earth (John 1:1, 14–18). Jesus' mission is to reveal the possibilities of heaven to those imprisoned in the world (John 1:31; 2:11; 3:21; 7:4; 9:3; 17:6; 21:1, 14). So Jesus doesn't just pass on information or make things clearer; rather, he brings the power and qualities of heaven into the world below, making it possible for people to experience love, light, truth, freedom, oneness, and salvation. In other words, humanity can be born again; they can leave behind a life defined as the "world" and begin to experience through Jesus the sphere of "heaven."

One of the most famous verses of the Bible explains how these things happen. "For God so loved the world that [God] gave

[God's] only Son, so that everyone who believes in him may not perish but may have eternal life" (John 3:16). In John's Gospel, Jesus invites the people to begin experiencing the qualities of life of heaven in the world as they believe in Jesus. However, to believe in Jesus is not an end in itself. It is how a person enmeshed in the world gains access in the present to important elements of heaven. As Jesus says, "Very truly, I tell you, whoever believes has eternal life" (John 6:47; e.g., 3:36; 5:24; 6:35; 10:38; 17:3).

When it comes to life beyond death, the Gospel of John criticizes an idea shared by many apocalyptic thinkers. After Lazarus died, Martha gave voice to the customary expectation, telling Jesus: "If you had been here, my brother would not have died. . . . [But] I know that he will rise again in the resurrection on the last day" (John 11:21, 24). Martha expects Lazarus will lie in the grave until the resurrection, but Jesus reinterprets what happens at death, declaring: "I *am* the resurrection and the life. Those who believe in me, even though they die, will live, and everyone who lives and believes in me will never die" (John 11:25–26). For John, those who believe in Jesus will experience eternal life in the present. When they die, they'll go on living, though in the heavenly sphere with Jesus.

John doesn't tell us what existence after death looks like for those who believe in Jesus, but his Gospel has similarities to the modified Platonism found in the Jewish philosophy of Philo. Therefore, looking at Philo can help us better understand John's expectations. For Philo, the soul (the nonmaterial aspect of the person) lives on after death, so Philo can say that some people study to attain "a higher existence immortal and incorporeal in the presence of [the one] who is . . . immortal and uncreated."[4] John likely has in mind a form of this way of thinking about how life continues after death.

John's Gospel presumes that a person experiences some form of immortality. However, the everlasting quality of life Jesus gives the believer in the world is superseded by what they experience in the next stage of life. As we read in John 14, Jesus has prepared a place for believers in God's house (heaven). Jesus says, "I will come again and will take you to myself, so that where I am, there you may be also" (John 14:3).

Some Christians regard the expression "I will come" in John 14:3, and similar statements in 14:18, 23, and 28, as references to Jesus returning in apocalyptic terms. That is, Jesus' return will be a public, cosmic event in which Jesus immediately transforms creation. However, nothing in the immediate context calls for this interpretation, nor does the larger perspective of the Gospel of John. While John's Gospel refers to a "last day" (John 6:39–40, 44, 54; 12:48), he may have in mind the idea that just as existence had a starting point (John 1:1–5), it will have an end point. In the meantime, the spheres of heaven and earth exist alongside one another without the expectation that history is moving toward a cataclysmic finale.

As we've seen by looking at the biblical story, we can't speak of *the* biblical perspective. In fact, the biblical authors don't regard the return of Jesus as the only way to imagine God's ultimate purposes. The Old Testament imagines God's final purposes taking place largely within this world. Most of the New Testament foresees the second coming of Jesus as the climactic end-time event through which God fulfills God's promises, though some of these promises will be fulfilled in the present age. The Gospel of John tends to emphasize believers experiencing heaven in the present, followed by a journey with Jesus to heaven after death.

While the viewpoints found in the Bible don't radically contradict one another, there are enough differences that we cannot simply paste them together. We also shouldn't take verses and passages out of their historical and literary contexts and use them as proof texts for what we would like to believe about the second coming. When we work with the biblical materials as we seek clarity about what we truly believe about the second coming, we should respect the diversity of the biblical voices and work with their distinct perspectives as we bring them into conversation with voices from church history and contemporary theological reflection.

SECTION TWO

"But I Thought the Church Had Always Believed . . ."

Voices from the History of the Church

In Section Two, we focus on the ways the churches' interpretations of God's purposes evolved from the end of the biblical era to the 1800s. Many of the apocalyptic elements found in the New Testament continued throughout Christian history. The churches also modified some elements and even set some aside. The original apocalyptic vision (often known as chiliasm, from a Greek word for "one thousand," a millennium) was adapted by the church as it took different forms and paths in the Eastern churches (Greek, Coptic, Syriac, Russian settings) and the Western churches (sometimes called the Latin churches).

Over time, the majority positions in both East and West tended to downplay the apocalyptic vision of the future. Nevertheless, apocalyptic movements continued to emerge with regularity, especially in the West. It should be noted that in the early centuries there was significant overlap between East and West. However, communication between East and West became less frequent, and the differences in theology and practice gradually became more pronounced after the fall of the Roman Empire in the West (fifth century CE) and the rise of Islam in the East (seventh century CE). Apocalyptic movements in the postbiblical world usually emerged either because the church felt threatened by oppression or due to a writer's perception that the church had become corrupt or lax in its life and practice.

It's important to remember that as Christianity took root in different contexts, it would bring elements present in the broader culture into its eschatological views. For example, both the church and the synagogue adapted elements from the Sibylline Oracles, a collection of sayings from priestesses (sybils) in the Roman era. Since the Sibylline Oracles broke world history into seven millenniums, by the fourth and fifth centuries CE, many Christians believed that the world was in the midst of the sixth millennium. If this is true, they reasoned, then Jesus' second coming should inaugurate the seventh millennium, which many believed would be an era of peace. This belief also lent itself to either reinforcing or challenging the "political theologies" of the day, that is, interpreting the Christian faith in such a way as to support the current political regime. We note instances of this phenomenon below.

We've chosen to lay out this journey through church history along two primary trajectories. (1) One trajectory focuses on how Eastern Christianity understood God's ultimate purposes beginning with Origen in the third century and taking the story to the immediate aftermath of the fall of Constantinople to the Ottomans (chapter 3). (2) Chapters 4 and 5 explore the Western trajectory beginning with Hippolytus in the third century and continuing through the medieval and renaissance periods to the Reformation and onward until we reach the nineteenth century. We'll explore developments after that period in chapters 6, 7, and 8, where we look at three primary interpretations of the millennium that began in the past but that continue into the present.

Background Common to the East and the West

Before we get to the three primary historical chapters, we set the stage by pointing out that during the second century CE many influential apocalyptic documents emerged that didn't make it into the New Testament canon (e.g., writings such as the *Shepherd of Hermas* and the *Apocalypse of Peter*). To the surprise of many Christians today, early churches were reluctant to include the book of Revelation in the Bible (in the canon) because of differences of opinion about what to make of its apocalyptic message. This uneasiness winds in and out of Christian communities for centuries. But two important figures offered millennialist views that help explain why the book of Revelation eventually made it into the canonical New Testament.

The first figure is Justin Martyr (c. 100–165 CE), who drew explicitly on the book of Revelation in his *Dialog with Trypho*. Justin believed that not only would Christ dwell in Jerusalem for a thousand years, but Christ would return very soon to destroy his enemies and set up his millennial kingdom. When Christ returned, the righteous would reign with him for a thousand years in the renewed Jerusalem, after which the final judgment would take place. Though Justin believed the end was near, he assumed that the reason for its delay was that the number of the righteous remained incomplete. Justin also believed that human souls would survive death until they would be reunited with their bodies on the day of judgment. This remained a common belief in the centuries to come and is still present in some churches today.

Irenaeus (c. 130–202 CE) came from Antioch in Syria but served as a bishop in Lyons (France). He is best known for his theological response to Gnosticism: *Adversus Haereses (Against Heresies)*. Gnosticism taught that the human body is evil and that secret knowledge—*gnosis* in Greek—was needed to liberate the soul from the body. In his response, Irenaeus appealed to the resurrection of the dead as a way of emphasizing the goodness of the material creation: God would resurrect the person as a *body*.

Irenaeus envisioned a two-part resurrection. At the first resurrection, the righteous in Christ would be raised to life and reign with Christ for a thousand years over a renewed earth (a restored Eden). He taught that Adam and Eve were created perfect but innocent. While God wanted them to mature into God's perfect vision for humanity (along with the rest of a perfect creation), things went awry (the fall). God then devised a rescue plan that included Jesus, whose life, death, and resurrection restored what was broken (recapitulation). During Christ's millennial reign, the righteous would experience what God had intended from the beginning for creation. However, Irenaeus didn't end there. He believed that after the thousand-year reign of the righteous, God would raise the rest of humanity to face God's judgment. The unrighteous would be cast into the fires of gehenna, while the righteous would enjoy God's blessings. What is important about Irenaeus's vision is that it was thoroughly material and not simply spiritual.

Churches in the East and the West Begin to Develop Different Emphases

As we move from the second into the third century, separate trajectories begin to emerge in the Eastern and Western portions of the emerging Christian world. There are many reasons why this took place.

In the East, Origen moved away from traditional apocalypticism and adapted ideas present in Greek and Roman culture to form a more spiritualized way of thinking about God's ultimate purposes that focused on the restoration of all things. Origen's position leans toward universal salvation—the idea that everyone would be saved. Origen envisioned union with God as one's ultimate destiny. In the West, the main body of the church ultimately followed Augustine and embraced a nonapocalyptic eschatology, though apocalyptic movements regularly popped up in both East and West.

While there are differences of emphasis, we notice similarities at points, ideas that emerged before the divisions that took place over time. Some of these ideas are enshrined in the creeds, including the confession found in the Apostles' Creed, which declared that after Christ was crucified, dead, and buried, "he descended into hell; the third day he rose again from the dead." This confession leads to the idea of Christ's "harrowing of hell," descending into the underworld after the crucifixion but before the resurrection to preach "to the spirits in prison" (1 Pet. 3:18–21).

In exploring the history of Christian eschatology, paying attention to context is important. As the churches in the East and West became more isolated from each other, they took on different visions of the future. Whether in the East or the West (or north or south), Christians have wrestled with what the future could look like, with most affirming the idea that something more exists beyond this life, even if Christians take separate perspectives on the nature of this life and how it will transpire.

3

A Path toward Universal Restoration

The Eastern Christian Church

Following the journeys of Paul and other early missionaries, the early Christian movement found homes throughout the empire. As the third century opened, there were attempts to tamp down apocalyptic expectations concerning the coming millennial reign of Christ. Figures such as Origen (184–253) and Augustine (354–430) offered spiritualized visions of the reign of Christ. Instead of thinking of Christ's millennial reign as a historical event, they envisioned it in spiritual terms, internal within a person. So, the mainstream vision often focused its attention on the internal reign of Christ, while the more apocalyptic visions were found among those living on the margins of society, a pattern that continues in some quarters into today.

In this chapter, we focus on Eastern Christianity. The leading churches in the East included Alexandria, Antioch, and later Constantinople (modern Istanbul). Among these churches, the book of Revelation was largely pushed to the side, at least until the fall of Constantinople in the fifteenth century. Eastern Christians tended to envision Jesus as the *Pantokrator* (omnipotent ruler) rather than as the crucified Christ. This vision of Jesus as the heavenly ruler became an important part of Byzantine (Eastern Roman Empire) political theology, as many Christians came to think of the eternal

Roman Empire as an expression of God's Realm on earth. The ruling Christ, they believed, authorized the rule of the emperor. It was only the fall of Constantinople in the fifteenth century that finally dashed these imperial eschatological visions.

Origen and the Restoration of All Things

A major contributor to this de-emphasis on apocalypticism was the third-century theologian Origen of Alexandria, Egypt. The Alexandrian church, unlike the Antiochian (Syrian) church, which tended to read Scripture more literally, followed Origen in embracing a more spiritual/allegorical perspective. Despite their differences in interpretation, theologians from both Antioch and Alexandria embraced what is often called "realized eschatology." That is, they taught, as we have noted, that the Realm of God is already occurring (being realized) in the present moment.

Origen was perhaps the most influential theologian between Paul and Augustine. He drew on Greek philosophy, especially Plato, to interpret Scripture. He emphasized allegorical/spiritual readings of Scripture over literal ones. In an allegorical reading, the literal (face-value) reading points to something spiritual in nature (think here of the parable of the Sower, in which each soil represents a different response to the message of the Realm; Mark 4:1–10; Matt. 13:1–23; Luke 8:4–15). Thus, when Origen read the apocalyptic texts, he interpreted them as spiritual symbols. When the book of Revelation spoke of the millennial reign of Christ, Origen did not expect a historical event. Instead, he envisioned Christ's reign as an inner spiritual experience. When he read New Testament texts such as Matthew 24–25 (Jesus' teaching on the last days), he saw them referring to false prophets, persecutions, and the depletion of the world's resources in every age, rather than as a literal prediction of events occurring in the last days. Therefore, Origen focused on what these passages said about the believer's ongoing spiritual growth or maturity. As for the second coming, Origen envisioned it as a present spiritual experience, not a future historical event.[1]

Following his spiritual interpretation of the second coming of Jesus, Origen also offered a spiritual reading of biblical references to the general resurrection (the moment when both the living and the dead are raised to life to face the day of judgment). His starting point, which was rooted in his philosophical beliefs, taught that when an individual died, their soul continued to exist, while the body decayed. When it comes to the resurrection of the body, Origen pointed to Paul's reference to a spiritual body in 1 Corinthians 15. In this scenario, the original physical body wouldn't be reconstituted. Instead, an individual would receive a new spiritual body that has continuity with the earthly body. That continuity is rooted in the ongoing existence of the immortal soul.

Perhaps Origen's most lasting legacy regarding last things is his belief that all things eventually will be restored to what God originally intended. This restoration includes not only the human creation but the universe itself. When it comes to judgment and punishment, Origen believed the unworthy would be punished, but he was unclear about the form punishment would take. Regardless of the form of such punishment, it wouldn't be eternal. Instead, he envisioned this punishment as a process of purification (refinement by fire), so that in the end everything would be restored to its intended purpose. The Greek word here is *apokatastasis* ("restoration"), which has come to signify for many the idea of universal salvation. For Origen, the final state is loving union with God.

It should be noted that not everyone embraced Origen's ideas. In fact, a later council condemned his perspective. Nevertheless, his teachings had already penetrated Christian theology through his heirs, including Athanasius, Gregory of Nyssa, John Climacus, and Maximus the Confessor. These thinkers further developed the idea of restoration so that Origen's vision lives on in the East to this day.

Origen's vision of restoration is compatible with the confession that after Jesus' death but before his resurrection, Jesus descended into Hades and liberated the souls of those inhabiting that realm. This idea is found in the Apostles' Creed, along with both canonical and noncanonical texts (e.g., Eph. 4:8–9; 1 Pet. 3:19–20). Second-century theologians such as Clement of Alexandria developed a fairly detailed vision of Christ's descent, following 1 Peter 3:18–21. Clement suggested that Christ addressed all those in hell who might believe in Christ. "If, then, the Lord descended into Hades for no other end but to preach the Gospel, as he did descend, it was either to preach the Gospel to all or to the Hebrews only. If, accordingly, to all, then all who believe shall be saved, though they may be of the Gentiles, on making their profession there."[2]

> Regarding the descent into Hades, Origen believed that Christ descended not only to preach but also to vanquish the devil by depriving the devil of power. However, that power will not be completely annihilated until the second coming. Thus, Origen wrote in his commentary on Romans: "By his death he destroyed him who possessed the power of death (*mortem imperium*), that is the devil, in order to liberate those held by death. For, having bound the strong man and having conquered him by the cross, he entered into his house, which is the house of death, or Hades, and spoiled his goods, that is liberated the souls which death held."[3]

Renouncing Worldly Things:
Ascetical (Self-Disciplining) Eschatology

The persecutions began to subside, as did the prospect of martyrdom in the late third and early fourth centuries. Some believers felt the need to pursue a more rigorous spiritual life. For some in the Syriac-speaking world (roughly Syria and Iraq) and in Egypt, this involved heading into the desert to live a life of simplicity as a hermit, renouncing all worldly things (asceticism). As these hermits deprived themselves of creature comforts in pursuit of a deeper spiritual experience, they often meditated on the prospect of experiencing either the joy of heaven or the horror of hell when they died. They often had vivid visions of spiritual warfare taking place between God and the devil or between angels and demons.

By engaging in these practices, which they saw as expressions of the Realm of God already present, they believed they could defeat the demonic elements that tried to entice them to stray from the path of faith through their ascetical practices. Such self-denial would make them worthy of paradise. Although there are apocalyptic elements to these experiences, the desert hermits understood these things to be internal spiritual battles that would perfect them in their journey of faith. While in the beginning these were solitary forays into the wilderness, eventually they would be institutionalized in monasticism.

> This ascetical vision—understood to be a means of preparing for life after death through a life of prayer—is expressed well by Diadochus of Photiki in Greece (fifth century CE): A person who is not detached from worldly cares can neither love God truly nor hate the devil as he should, for such cares are both a burden and a veil. His intellect cannot discern the tribunal which will judge him, neither can it foresee the verdict which will be given at his trial. For all these reasons, then, withdrawal from the world is invaluable.[4]

These ascetical writers from St. Antony to Diadochus envisioned a path to God in the present by embracing a form of realized eschatology. Thus, their focus was not on the end times or the second coming, but on the possibility of experiencing heavenly life in the present through a focus that came about through self-denial, with the fullness of heaven coming only after death.

Gregory of Nyssa Advocates Universal Salvation

In the fourth and fifth centuries in the East, the theological debates in the church focused on Jesus' identity and the nature of the Trinity. These debates led to the creation of several creedal statements, including the Nicene Creed and the definition of Chalcedon. As for the future state, the creeds, as Gregory Riley notes, affirmed the premise that Jesus "would one day judge the living and the dead and would be the king in a kingdom that would have no end; there would be a resurrection and there would be life in the coming age. The character of each of these beliefs—what *kind* of kingdom or resurrection or future life—was left to the individual Christian or teacher or local church to determine."[5]

Nevertheless, while there was little discussion of the second coming of Jesus and the end of times, there was discussion of the nature of the afterlife. Among those who contributed to the conversation was Gregory of Nyssa (fourth century CE). (The city of Nyssa was in the district of Cappadocia, located in what is now Turkey.) Among the topics this Cappadocian theologian took up was the prospect of universal salvation. More specifically, Gregory further developed Origen's work on the restoration of all things. This was important because Origen's theology had been deemed problematic by some in the church. However, since Gregory was considered fully orthodox, he could make the doctrine of the restoration of all things acceptable to later Christians.

Gregory develops his vision of the future in *On the Soul and the Resurrection,* which takes the form of a dialogue with his sister Macrina after the death of their brother Basil of Caesarea (in what is now Turkey). They focus their attention on the question of whether the soul survives death and how it might be reunited with the body. The answer they offer is that at the resurrection the elements that make up the body, though scattered, will be brought together according to the pattern of the soul, which survives death as an immaterial essence. Before the soul is reunited with the body, it will be purified, as gold is refined. This process of purification separates good from evil by "pulling the soul towards the fellowship of blessedness. It is the tearing apart of what has grown together which brings pain to the one who is being pulled. The level of pain is proportionate to the amount of evil present in a person."[6] Evil must be fully removed from the person so that the soul might be free, and God might be all in all.

Gregory envisioned the resurrection of the body involving the restoration of the person to their original state. Thus, with the resurrection, the person "no longer has its life ordered by its natural properties but goes over into a spiritual and immutable state (for it is characteristic of the physical body to be continuously altered from what it is and to be always changing into something different). Of those excellent qualities which we see now shared by human beings along with plants and animals, none will be left in the life hereafter."[7]

So, Gregory concludes that "when such things are cleansed and purified away by the treatment through fire, each of the better qualities will enter in their place: incorruptibility, life, honor, grace, glory, power, and whatever else of this kind we recognize in God Himself and in His image, which is our human nature."[8] Thus, death is therapeutic and healing. In his *Catechetical Discourse*, Gregory distinguishes between those who have been purified through the mystical waters of baptism and those without baptism, who must experience purifying fire.[9] Gregory does not offer a fully developed universalist perspective. However, his line of thought does move in that direction.

Maximus the Confessor and Union with God

One of the key developments in Eastern theology is the belief that humanity's ultimate destiny, and perhaps that of creation itself, is union with God. In the fourth century, Athanasius of Alexandria (in Egypt) suggested that in the incarnation God became human so that humans could become God. This concept is known as *theosis* (deification or divinization). Maximus the Confessor (580–662 CE), whose work centered in Constantinople (modern Istanbul), developed further an idea that has roots in Origen, Athanasius, and Gregory of Nyssa. While it hints at universal salvation, Brian Daley notes that the "final divinization of rational creatures will only be realized in those who have shown themselves worthy of God's gift." Thus, "each person remains free to frustrate the achievement of God's saving purpose in himself by refusing to follow the way of Christ."[10] Maximus believed that the ascetic and contemplative life provided the best pathway to divinization. As Maximus developed this idea of deification, he spoke of a process in which believers become "participants of the divine nature" (2 Pet. 1:4), and thus they would be "sharers in His eternity, and so . . . might come to be like Him through deification by grace [cf. 1 John 3:2]. It is through deification that all things are reconstituted and achieve their permanence; and it is for its sake that what is not is brought into being and given existence."[11] Maximus hoped that in the end all things might be restored, and thus all rational creatures would experience deification; but he left the possibility that not all would embrace the way of God.

The Reemergence of Apocalypticism in the East

For a significant period, there was little interest in eschatology among Eastern Christians, who were more focused on other theological concerns, such as the Trinity and how Christ could be both human and divine. Things began to change in the sixth century. While the Western Roman Empire had fallen in the fifth century, the empire in the East still seemed strong. The sixth century was the era of Justinian (who ruled 527–565), who sought to take back territory in the West lost to Germanic invasions and reunite the Eastern church with Rome.

Despite his success in expanding the empire and in building great monuments such as the church known as the Hagia Sophia in Constantinople (now Istanbul), Justinian's reign saw significant turmoil. Interestingly, Justinian envisioned his calling as emperor in eschatological terms, believing that God had called him to cleanse the empire of heresy and paganism and reunite the church in preparation for the second coming of Jesus at the end of the age. His efforts sought to purge from the empire not only paganism but also non-Chalcedonian churches. This led some Christian opponents to view him as the antichrist.

Justinian envisioned his reign in terms expressed in the Tiburtine Sibyl, a key fourth-century apocalyptic text. The Tiburtine Sibyl, which followed the model of the ancient Greek and Roman Sibylline Oracles, provided a Christianized authorization for the imperial office. It demonstrates how Christian apocalyptic writers borrowed from the larger culture to provide a foundation for its evolving imperial theology, which sought to present God as ordaining the emperor and the empire. The Sibyl spoke of the Last Roman Emperor, who would rise at the end of the age and restore the Christian empire to greatness as a precursor to the second coming. This emperor would defeat the enemies of the Christian faith, establish righteousness on earth, and then travel to Jerusalem to hand over the crown to Christ as he returned in glory.

The Tiburtine Sibyl is only one expression of the rising apocalypticism that emerged in the sixth century and extended into the eighth century. This was partly due to the presence of a prominent and widespread millennialist understanding of earth history that envisioned earth history lasting for seven millennia. If, as many believed, the third-century church leader Hippolytus was correct in asserting that the sixth millennium would end in the year 500, that meant the seventh and final millennium had already begun, so Christ's second coming must be imminent.

We see here an excellent illustration of the importance of taking historical context into account when interpreting ancient thinking about the second coming. The millennial vision we have just discussed was compounded by the pressure put on the borders of the Eastern Roman Empire. First, there is the rise in Arabia of Islam, which quickly spread into the Christian heartland of Syria, Palestine, and Mesopotamia. This was compounded by the pressure put on the empire's northern borders by the Goths and to the east by the Persians (who would soon convert to Islam).

Thus, apocalyptic theories such as the story of the Last Roman Emperor (mentioned above) gave comfort and hope to the empire's residents. Surely the empire would continue until Christ returned. The legend of the Last Emperor, taken together with speculation that the Byzantine Empire might be the fourth and final empire of Daniel's vision (Dan. 7:7–8, 23–24), suggested that the empire was sacred. Indeed, many people envisioned Rome as the force restraining the antichrist (2 Thess. 2:6–7). Even theologians who didn't identify Rome with Daniel's vision identified the empire with the Realm of God.

One of the events of the seventh century that gave Eastern Christians pause was the Byzantine Empire's loss of territory to the Persians, including Syria and Palestine. The year 614 was especially significant. In that year the Persians not only took control of Jerusalem, but they took possession of the sacred relic of the true cross, that is, the cross on which Jesus was crucified. The legend of the true cross goes back to Constantine, whose mother, Helena, is said to have discovered the sacred relic in the Holy Land. Cyril of Jerusalem (fourth century CE) promoted the legend, drawing pilgrims to the Church of the Holy Sepulchre. The legend of the Last Roman Emperor came into play when the Byzantine emperor Heraclius recaptured Syria and Palestine and restored the true cross to Jerusalem. This gave birth to the belief that Heraclius could be the Last Emperor, therefore raising the question of whether this was a sign that the second coming was imminent.

This hope was short-lived, because a truly apocalyptic moment emerged as Islamic armies swept out of Arabia, capturing Syria, Palestine, and Jerusalem. Among the first to give voice to an apocalyptic interpretation of the Arab conquest was Maximus the Confessor. While his letter concerning Islam is marked by anti-Jewish views, we want to take notice of his apocalyptic description of "this barbarous people from the desert overrunning another's lands as if they were their own! And to see this civilized polity devoured by savage and raging beasts, who have the mere appearance of only the form of human beings!" He also spoke of Jewish people believing that they were serving God by "doing what is hated by God" in welcoming the enemy forces and making way for "the advent of the evil one and revealing by what they are doing the arrival of the Antichrist, since they ignored the true Savior."[12]

Apocalypticism and Islam

Islam was born in the seventh century CE as an apocalyptic movement with Muhammad claiming to be God's final prophet. Later biographies of Muhammad downplay the eschatological elements of his message. While the *Qur'an* is largely ahistorical, it does give evidence that Muhammad believed the end of the age was imminent (*Qur'an* 22:7). Indeed, the *Qur'an* reveals that Muhammad believed the final judgment was coming soon and that he would play a key role in preparing for that day. As Stephen Shoemaker writes, "Muhammad thus appears as a monotheist prophet within the Abrahamic tradition who called his followers to renounce polytheism, to submit to the divine laws, and to prepare themselves for the impending doom: altogether, it is a portrait rather familiar from the Jewish and Christian scriptures."[13]

The *Qur'an* describes Muhammad's victory over the Quraysh at Badr (in present-day Saudi Arabia) in 624, which proved to be the turning point in his prophetic career, in apocalyptic terms. The *Qur'an* speaks of God sending three thousand angels to assist in this battle for control of Arabia (*Qur'an* 3:123–125).[14] Thus, as the *Qur'an* reveals: "And you did not kill them, but it was Allah who killed them. And you threw not, [O Muhammad], when you threw, but it was Allah who threw that He might test the believers with a good test. Indeed, Allah is Hearing and Knowing" (*Qur'an* 8:17).[15]

While Muhammad may have had an apocalyptic understanding of his calling, later Islamic theology placed Jesus at the center of its vision of the coming day of judgment. Muhammad might be Islam's final prophet of Islam, but the second coming of Jesus served as the precursor to the emergence of the messiah at the end of the age.

Christians need to understand the important role Jesus plays in Islam, including the role played by his second advent. While Muslims and Christians differ in their belief systems regarding Jesus, he plays an essential role in vintage Islamic eschatology. Although references to the second coming of Jesus are not found directly in the *Qur'an*, the hadiths (the sayings of Muhammad) reveal that at the end of the age, the *Mahdi* (messiah) will appear, and he will be accompanied by Jesus. Together they will defeat the antichrist and restore Islam to its purest state. After this, Jesus will help convert Christians and Jews to the truth (as understood by Islam).

With this vision driving Islam, Jews and Christians struggled to make sense of it. Christians feared his movement, while some Jews saw him and his successors as their redeemers. Jews who welcomed the rise of Islam saw Islam as the way God would mete out judgment on the oppressive Christian Byzantine Empire. Many Syriac-speaking Christians, who also suffered under the Byzantines, envisioned the rise of Islam as a sign of divine judgment on the Byzantines, and many converted to Islam.

For these Christians, the question arose as to whether this was a moment of freedom or preparation for the end of the age. The seventh-century Syriac text the *Apocalypse of Pseudo-Methodius* answered the question by suggesting the Arab conquest was a sign that the end of the world was near. However, this day would not occur before the king of the Greeks (the Byzantine emperor) turned back the Muslim threat. Then,

> there will be peace on earth the like of which there has not been before, because it is the last peace of the end of the world. And there will be joy on the whole earth and men will dwell in great peace, and the churches will be restored, and the cities will be rebuilt, and the priests will be freed from tax, and priests and men will recover at that time from labor and weariness and exhaustion. . . . And this was in fulfillment of the words of Jesus that a great peace would come upon the earth.[16]

Islam would continue to influence apocalyptic and eschatological conversation for centuries to come, as the Byzantine Empire further contracted, while Jesus' return to restore order was delayed. Thus, the empire would fall, and the Last Emperor would fail to appear. This led to disappointment among many Greek-speaking Christians.

This general pattern had already occurred in history. A particular people, informed by the apocalyptic impulses in their culture, came to think that their moment in history was the apocalypse.

They looked toward this moment in history with a sense of hope, but these hopes were frustrated when it did not occur in their historical moment. This pattern will repeat itself time and again, continuing to the present day.

Gregory Palamas and Participating in the Divine Nature

Even as the Byzantine Empire fell apart so that many Eastern churches found themselves living under Islamic (primarily Ottoman) rule, theological developments continued, especially concerning more spiritual matters. With this in mind, we turn to Gregory Palamas, a fourteenth-century monk known for his defense of *hesychasm* (a monastic movement seeking union with God through contemplation and prayer). Gregory further developed the concept of *theosis* (deification/divinization).

Palamas's theological works are rooted in the works of figures we have discussed in this book: Maximus the Confessor, Gregory of Nyssa, and ultimately Origen. In defending *hesychasm* as a pathway to deification (union with God) through asceticism and contemplation, Palamas developed his vision of God's nature. In doing so, he distinguished between God's essence (transcendent and unknowable) and God's uncreated energies (knowable). God's essence is God's transcendent being, which human beings cannot perceive in its purity. God's energies—as the designation implies—offer a way for human beings to actually experience God's activity in the world. Human beings cannot fully approach God's essence, but by participating in and with God's energies, human beings can experience union with God or deification (*theosis*). For Palamas, deification can be humanity's ultimate destiny. While he focused on *theosis* as humanity's ultimate destiny, he also affirmed his belief, laid out in his debates with his Turkish captors, that Christ would return to judge the world.

By distinguishing between God's essence and energies, Palamas envisions humanity's ultimate destiny as union with God, without absorption into God's essence. Those who experience deification by participating in God's nature don't lose their individual identity, but they experience immortality (deification). This vision of union with God remains an important feature of modern Orthodox theology and is finding homes outside Orthodoxy as well.

Apocalyptic Readings of the Fall of Constantinople

In 1453 everything changed, when Constantinople (Istanbul) fell to the Ottomans (who practiced Islam). Byzantine imperial theology assumed the empire would endure until the rise of the Last Emperor, who would give sovereignty over the empire to Jesus, who would return and reign for a thousand years. While many viewed Constantinople as the inheritor of Augustus's Roman Empire, they also envisioned the city as the New Jerusalem. The Hagia Sophia, the giant cathedral built in the sixth century, was seen as the temple of this New Jerusalem. This church was built square to represent the earth, with the dome representing heaven. Thus, in Byzantium, heavenly and earthly kingdoms merged. This is the political theology we mentioned earlier in its extreme form. Now this ideology that undergirded the Eastern church's self-understanding collapsed.

There had been cracks in this vision for some time. The sack of Constantinople by the Crusaders in 1204 raised questions about the empire's long-term viability. Then in the fourteenth century, Muslim Turks and Tartars began to encroach on the city. This led to the rise of more negative apocalyptic visions as the fifteenth century began. Although imperial theology continued to hold, it had begun to fray. When the city fell in 1453, many Greeks assumed that the end of the world had come.

This unexpected turn of events required theological explanations, and most of these explanations were apocalyptic. On the one hand, some saw the new world as one of promise, delivered by the victorious Turks. Other apocalyptic thinkers suggested that the city fell to a Muslim army, not because of the superiority of the Ottoman armies, but because of the sins of the city's people. Others adopted the view similar to one envisioned by the book of Daniel, namely, that empires rise and fall, and such was the case with Byzantium.

The fall of Constantinople rocked the Christian world and created fodder for apocalyptic visions. Orthodox Christianity had spread into eastern Europe in the ninth and tenth centuries, eventually reaching the Viking ruler of Kiev (Kyiv—Ukranian spelling), Prince Vladimir (956–1015), whose conversion set in motion the creation of what has become the Russian Orthodox Church. After the fall of Constantinople, the question raised in the East was, Who would carry on the Byzantine vision? As we have seen so often, politics and religion went hand in hand.

While there were several claimants, Moscow, though a Mongol vassal state, claimed the mantle as the Third Rome and thus the legitimate successor to the Byzantine church. The administrative center of the Russian church moved from Kyiv to Moscow at the time of the fall of Constantinople, following the ruling princes, who also made such a move. To cement the relationship between Moscow and Constantinople, Russian grand prince Ivan III (1440–1505) married Sophia, the niece of the last Byzantine emperor. The rise of the Russian church, and its claim to be the Third Rome, provided the foundation for Russian nationalism.

This linkage between the Russian state and the church continued to develop, with Moscow claiming not only that it was the heir of Constantinople, but also that true Christianity survived only with this church. This claim was rooted in "The Tale of the White Cowl," which originated in Novgorod in western Russia. According to the story, a white cowl had been passed down from the apostles through the pope, and then, after the apostasy of the Western church, it passed to the church at Constantinople after an angel miraculously preserved it. Then after a warning that Constantinople would fall to the Muslims, the cowl was passed on to the archbishop of Novgorod. The myth surrounding it suggested that as long as the Russian church preserved the cowl, it would stand out as the leading Christian nation.

This apocalyptic story led Ivan IV to transform the Russian church, seeking to make it the leading Christian church. Ivan took the title tsar (czar) as a nod to his affirmation that Moscow was the true heir of the Byzantines and the leading Orthodox church in the world and claimant to oversight of the larger Russian world, including Ukraine.[17] We see here an instance of the politician (the tsar) co-opting religion to shore up the authority of the state, something that occurs again and again in history. While Russia sought to lay claim to Constantinople's legacy, Orthodoxy is quite diverse in its geography, language, and practices.

When it comes to eschatology (last things), the expectation that goes back to Origen is that the ultimate destiny of creation is rooted in the belief that there will be a final restoration of all things. Perhaps Orthodox theologian Andrew Louth provides a suitable summary until we come to our discussion of modern Orthodox eschatology in Section Four:

> But for Eastern Orthodoxy it is in prayer and worship of God that our faith is defined and refined: a God who created the world and loves it, whose love is expressed in his identifying himself with his creation, and especially the human creation, made in his image, through the Incarnation and the cross, a love that is manifested in its transfiguring power through the resurrection. The centrality of prayer and worship prevents us from narrowing down our faith to some human construction, however magnificent.[18]

4

Settling In for the Long Haul

Views of the Second Coming in the Christian West

C hristianity in the Latin-speaking West often took different forms than in the East. Because most of our readers are heirs of this Western tradition, we've divided this conversation into two chapters. Chapter 4 focuses on the period 200 CE to 1500 CE, while chapter 5 takes the story from the Reformation in the sixteenth century up to the eighteenth.

Third- and Fourth-Century Trends

We begin with Hippolytus of Rome (170–235), Tertullian (160–220), and Cyprian (210–258). Both Tertullian and Cyprian resided in Carthage (modern Tunisia). These three third-century church leaders provided the foundations for Western understandings of the future. There is a significant continuity between the views of these theologians and those of Irenaeus. Hippolytus is important to this conversation because he laid down the foundation for the views of the second coming that developed over the next several centuries. For example, he wrote the earliest complete commentary on Daniel, while suggesting that the second coming might not be on the immediate horizon. As he studied apocalyptic texts such as Daniel, he concluded that Christ was born in the middle of the sixth millennium of world history. If this was true, then the second coming still lay several centuries in the future. By his calculations, the end would come five hundred years after the birth of Jesus. That placed the second coming some three hundred years in Hippolytus's future.

Hippolytus laid out his vision of the end of days in two important documents. Besides his commentary on Daniel, he wrote a brief exposition of the biblical texts dealing with the last days, including Daniel and Revelation, titled *On Christ and Antichrist.* He opined that the antichrist would mimic the Son of God: even as "Christ is a lion, so Antichrist is also a lion; Christ is a king, so Antichrist is also a king. The Saviour was manifested as a lamb; so he too, in like manner, will appear as a lamb, though within he is a wolf."[1] Hippolytus read Daniel and Revelation through a spiritualized, nonliteral lens.

Tertullian is much better known to modern readers than Hippolytus. While Hippolytus resided in Rome, Tertullian lived in Carthage in North Africa. Tertullian's eschatology drew from Justin and Irenaeus, as well as the Montanists, a movement that began in Asia Minor and gained prominence in North Africa during the third century. Brian Daley points out that "for Tertullian, the coming end of history is above all to be a time of reckoning: the settling of accounts between God and those who have come to deserve reward or punishment." Unlike Hippolytus, perhaps influenced by the Montanists, Tertullian believed the emergence of the antichrist was imminent. Therefore, "as part of his polemic against both skeptical pagans and dualist Gnostics, Tertullian emphasizes that Christians look forward to a universal resurrection when the material body of every person will rise again to share in the reward or punishment of its soul."[2] Unlike Origen, his contemporary in Alexandria, Tertullian gave judgment a central role in his apocalyptic theology, rather than restoration of all things.

When it comes to the afterlife, Tertullian envisioned an interim state between death and resurrection on the day of judgment. He imagined Hades being a large subterranean space that serves as a reception area for the dead. He draws on the parable of the

Rich Man and Lazarus and the tradition that Jesus descended into Hades after his death (Luke 16:19–31). In this state, the dead experience a foretaste of what is to come, either punishment or consolation. Thus, Hades was divided into two regions, separating the good from the wicked (as in the parable).

Montanism was a prophetic movement that emerged in Asia Minor (western Turkey today) around 170. While there's no evidence the Montanists were theologically unorthodox or their apocalyptic visions were out of line with other common views, they were deemed controversial because of their anti-institutionalism. Additionally, they emphasized the role of the Spirit as the giver of revelation and featured women prophets at a time when the participation of women in Christian leadership was discouraged. Montanists expected that Christ would soon return to set up a literal millennial reign and that Christ would return to the Phrygian village of Pepuza (in western Turkey). From Phrygia, Montanists quickly spread across North Africa. Their commitment to preparing themselves for Jesus' return led them to embrace martyrdom. Among those martyrs was Perpetua, whose story has continued to attract attention.

Cyprian of Carthage served as bishop of that important North African church during the persecutions of Decius and Valerian in the mid-third century. Cyprian followed Hippolytus's interpretation of Christ's return, but since he placed Adam's creation a hundred years earlier than Hippolytus, he moved up the timing of the end of the age by a century. Persecutions and a plague occurring during this period led him to believe the end of the age was close at hand. Therefore, he promised his flock that if they remained faithful, even unto death (though not necessarily martyrdom), they would gain immediate entrance into the Realm of God. In making this promise Cyprian moved beyond his predecessors, who limited this promise to the martyrs.

The persecutions experienced by early Christians raised important questions. If, following Cyprian, faithfulness even under duress served as the hallmark of the Christian life, then what happens if a person denies their faith to save their life?

Could this be the unpardonable sin? What happens if clergy deny the faith? Would the sacraments they performed be considered invalid? These questions became the fodder for schism and theological developments, especially after the persecutions ended with Constantine's Edict of Toleration in 313.

A Christian leader from North Africa named Donatus taught that if clergy denied the faith, this invalidated the sacraments over which they officiated. Not only that, but the churches they served were apostate. The Donatist church emerged during a disputed episcopal election in Carthage. Donatus insisted that anyone baptized by lapsed clergy should be rebaptized, rooting the validity of the sacrament in the holiness of the priest. This led to a schism in Carthage and the birth of a separate Donatist church that had a long history in North Africa.

North Africa took a central role in the next chapters of the discussion of the last things, by way of conflict between the Donatists and Augustine. While the Donatists didn't focus on the millennium itself, they did have a strong sense that the end of the age was near at hand. A central element of their eschatology was their self-identification as a remnant church. They insisted they were the only true church in North Africa. Believing that the gospel had been proclaimed to the nations and the larger church had apostatized, they would faithfully wait as the remnant church for the coming end of the age. Although the Donatists weren't millennialists, they were a dissident religious and social movement. The Donatists were strongly represented among the more rural Berber population, while the mainstream church was found among the more Romanized elite. Their apocalyptic (though not millennialist) perspective focused on creating a pure, visible church in preparation for the end of the age and the return of Christ.

Augustine's Spiritualized Eschatology

Augustine of Hippo (354–430) sought to defend the mainstream church against the charge of apostasy raised by the Donatists and others. This was a highly chaotic period within the Western

Roman Empire. Germanic tribes had crossed the Danube and Rhine Rivers into imperial territory, weakening imperial control over its western provinces. Some Christians speculated that these tribes might be biblical Gog and Magog. When Alaric and his Visigoth army sacked Rome in 410, and the Vandals invaded North Africa in 429 (a year before Augustine's death), many in the empire believed the end of the age had dawned.

Although this chaotic state of affairs was part of Augustine's reality, he chose to embrace a spiritualized millennial vision of history rather than an apocalyptic one. He rejected the idea that the destiny of secular kingdoms, like the Roman Empire, and God's plan of salvation were intertwined. He insisted that current events shouldn't be read into apocalyptic texts. That included the sack of Rome. In his view, these texts referred to the inner struggle within the human soul between good and evil. He cautioned against trying to determine the timing of Christ's return and the final consummation.

Interestingly, the Donatist theologian Tyconius (d. 380) offered a similar interpretation in his commentary on Revelation. Tyconius interpreted the millennial promise of Revelation 20 as a reference to the church. As a Donatist, he envisioned a purified church that faced persecution. By embracing a nonliteral interpretation of the millennium, Tyconius offered his own form of realized eschatology. He believed that the focus should be on creating a purified institutional church in preparation for Christ's eventual return. As Brian Daley notes, for Tyconius and the Donatists, "the need to purify and extend the institutional Church is all the more vital, because the time left for doing it is so short."[3]

Although Augustine and Tyconius differed on many points, Augustine drew upon Tyconius's nonliteral interpretation of the millennium. The latter embraced a broad vision that puts little emphasis on determining the moment of Christ's return and more emphasis on spiritually experiencing Christ in the present. Indeed, the Donatists sought to create a purified church in the present. Like Tyconius, Augustine equated the millennium with the church age. According to Brian Daley, for Augustine, the eschaton involves "the end of history itself and the beginning of the 'eternal Sabbath,' when God, who is beyond all time and all temporal succession, will 'rest in us'" (*Confessions* 13.37).[4] Augustine believed that a definite moment would come when God would end the current world and fully manifest salvation, but human beings could not know anything about when or how that change would take place.

Augustine also de-emphasized the duration of the millennium, something he passed on to his theological heirs. Writing after the sack of Rome, in his *The City of God,* Augustine borrowed from 2 Peter 3:8, which suggested that with God "one day is like a thousand years, and a thousand years are like one day." So, when Augustine spoke of world history taking place according to a six-thousand-year time frame, followed by a Sabbath of a thousand years, he didn't understand these things in literal terms. Instead, he envisioned them as spiritual epochs of varying lengths.

When Augustine read Revelation, the central idea he took from it was that the strong man (the devil) who held humanity captive would be bound and thrown into the abyss.[5] As for the reign of the saints with Christ, this began at the time of Jesus' first advent. Therefore, the Realm of God is concurrent with the age of the church.[6] The ultimate hope for those who believed in Christ was that they would experience the promised rest, the eternal Sabbath that comes from God, at the time and in the way orchestrated by God and unknown to human beings until that time.

While the Donatists sought to create a purified church in the current age, Augustine distinguished between the earthly church, in which wheat and tares existed side by side, and the heavenly church, composed of the fully redeemed. These two churches would exist in parallel until Christ returned to inaugurate the eternal Sabbath. This idea comes up several times in Christian history.

By embracing a nonliteral vision of the millennium, Augustine could turn his attention to the personal experience of divine judgment and salvation. For him, and thus for those who followed him, the eschatological hope was not to be found in some historical catastrophe. Rather, it would be found in experiencing the resurrection in the present. Augustine embraced the idea that at death the body would separate from the soul. The latter would ascend to the heavenly realm, until the day of judgment, when body and soul would reunite. Responding to questions about the nature of the resurrected body, Augustine taught that at the moment of the resurrection one would be restored to the stature achieved at their prime, which for Augustine was around the age of thirty.[7]

This nonliteral interpretation of the millennium became the official view of the Roman Catholic Church for the next thousand years. Thus it set aside the expectation that Christ would return before the millennium to set up a subsequent millennial kingdom. In place of this way of thinking, the church offered a symbolic millennium that was embodied by the church.

Apocalyptic Movements (400–1500)

Although Augustine's spiritualized eschatology became the dominant position within the institutional church, apocalyptic movements still erupted with some frequency. Islamic forces swept through North Africa and into Spain, causing great concern among Christians. North Africa, once among the most Christianized regions of the Roman Empire, with Alexandria, Carthage (in modern Tunisia), and later Hippo (in Algeria) being important centers of Christian life and theological development, fell to Islamic invaders during the seventh and eighth centuries. Many other invaders troubled the empire. Viking raiders afflicted Christianized portions of northern Europe and Britain, as evidenced in the destruction of the famed abbey at Lindisfarne in northeast England in 793. The Magyars came from the east, wreaking social havoc on Christian Europe. Unlike in North Africa, where Islam came to dominate, by the year 1000, the Magyars in Hungary and the population of the Scandinavian nations had largely converted to Christianity. Nevertheless, these realities contributed to religious anxiety and interest in apocalyptic visions, especially as

Christian Europe moved toward the year 1000. Could these chaotic developments be signs that the end was near?

The eleventh century proved to be a time of increased apocalyptic ferment, in large part connected to conflict with Muslim rulers in the Middle East. Until around 1050 the Arab rulers of Jerusalem and the Holy Land permitted largely unrestricted pilgrimage to holy sites, but then the Seljuk Turks conquered the region and brought most of the pilgrimages to a halt.

This set the stage for the First Crusade. Pope Urban II embraced the crusading movement, in part because of millennialism. In his sermon calling for a crusade against the Muslim rulers of the Holy Land, Urban spoke of the Christian reconquest of Jerusalem as a precursor to the second coming. Millennialism may not have been the sole motivation for the first crusade, but it likely contributed to the capture of Jerusalem in 1099. After they took the city, the crusaders massacred both Jews and Muslims, considering the latter to be enemies of God. Crusaders would continue to draw on apocalyptic themes to justify their efforts.

One of the most important medieval apocalyptic movements in the West is connected to Joachim of Fiore (1135–1202). Joachim had a conversion experience during a pilgrimage to Jerusalem, after which he chose to live as a hermit, engage in lay preaching, and later enter the Benedictine monastery of Corazzo, Italy, which elected him as their abbot. Joachim's apocalyptic teachings brought him fame. These teachings proved influential long after his death. His apocalypticism emerged out of a series of visions that inspired his belief that the end of the age was imminent. This led him to begin preaching a message of penance. While he realized most people wouldn't heed his message, he believed that a remnant would remain faithful and receive their reward.

Joachim rooted his apocalyptic views in his Trinitarian theology. He envisioned three ages, which he pictured as three interlocking circles: the age of the Father (Old Testament), the age of the Son (the age of the church), and the age of the Spirit (the coming age when a holier and purer church would emerge). He believed the antichrist (most likely an antipope) was already living in Rome and would soon be revealed. The defeat of the antichrist would lead to the start of the age of the Spirit, but not before the church experienced a period of persecution. In his *Book of Figures* Joachim drew on the image of the seven-headed dragon of Revelation to describe seven major persecutions of the church. The sixth, and most recent, persecution of the church was the conquest of Jerusalem by Saladin, an Islamic leader (1187). The rise of the antichrist would lead to the seventh persecution.

Joachim drew his view of the antichrist from Daniel 8:23–24, which says that "a king of bold countenance shall arise, skilled in intrigue. He shall grow strong in power, shall cause fearful destruction, and shall succeed in what he does." This final antichrist is the one known as Gog.[8] Joachim responded to this vision of the antichrist by embracing monasticism as the means through which the church would remain faithful. He envisioned two orders of "spiritual men" through whom the church would stand against the forces of the antichrist: an order of preachers and an order of contemplative hermits. The rise of these orders would lead to the age of the Spirit.

A generation after Joachim, some Franciscans and Dominicans envisioned themselves fulfilling the monastic dimensions of Joachim's vision of the monastic utopia that would lead the resistance to the antichrist. The Spiritual Franciscans of the late thirteenth and early fourteenth centuries embraced Joachim's apocalyptic theology, along with other rigorist Franciscans. Joachim's identification of the antichrist with an antipope contributed to antipapalism among the Spiritual Franciscans.

Another follower of Joachim's apocalypticism was Peter Olivi (c. 1248–98), a theologian affiliated with the University of Paris. Olivi taught that Joachim's forty-two generations leading to the end of the second age began in the year 40 CE, when Peter became bishop of Rome. Thus, the end of that second age would take place in the year 1300. Olivi also envisioned two sets of seven ages, one related to the Old Testament and the second to the New Testament. He believed that the second set of ages began with Christ; Francis of Assisi, acting as the new Elijah, inaugurated the sixth age, the age of renewal connected with the Spiritual Franciscans. The church declared Olivi's works to be heretical after his death in 1298, which led to opposition to Pope John XII and the belief, among the rigorists, that the pope was the antichrist.

Other millennialist movements emerged in the fourteenth century. Though most were quietist, some turned to violence. The Black Death that struck Europe in the mid-fourteenth century contributed to the rise of apocalypticism, which linked the plague to the woes prophesied in Revelation. Many of these movements taught that the Parousia (second coming) was near. These movements included the Flagellants, who traveled about whipping themselves as signs of public penitence, hoping that their efforts would deter God's wrath.

5

Still Here after All These Years

Views of the Second Coming
in the Reformation and Beyond

The two centuries preceding the sixteenth century were a time of ferment. This period included the move of the papacy from Rome to Avignon (France), placing the papacy under French control, the so-called Babylonian Captivity of the church (1309–76). The end of the Babylonian Captivity led to the Great Schism (1378–1417), a period that featured two popes, one in Rome and one in Avignon. Each of these popes claimed the allegiance of different European states. The schism ended with the two rival popes being deposed and Martin V being elected in their place at the Council of Constance (1414–18). Later in the century, the last remnants of the Roman Empire collapsed with the fall of Constantinople. This was coupled with the beginnings of the Renaissance and the launch of the age of discovery. Thus, the Christian world was ripe for change.

On the Eve of the Reformation

As the fifteenth century ended, Ferdinand and Isabella ended Muslim presence in Spain and funded Columbus's voyages, which led to European colonial expansion in the Americas. This led to the genocide of indigenous peoples and the transport of enslaved Africans to the Americas. While the Ottomans expanded their control in the East, Christendom pushed westward.

Our story begins with the story of an apocalyptic preacher named Girolamo Savonarola (1452–98) who rose to power in the city of Florence, Italy, in the final decade of the fifteenth century. Savonarola was a Dominican priest who called for the cleansing of the Roman church and Italy using apocalyptic language. The target of his preaching was Pope Alexander VI (Rodrigo Borgia). His call for reform coincided with the decision of the French king, Charles VIII, to invade Italy (1494). Charles's invasion was spurred by astrological guidance hailing him as the new Charlemagne. Charles spared Florence, but the invasion led to the eviction of the Medicis from power, enabling Savonarola to fill the power vacuum in Florence. Savonarola began to create his New Jerusalem, a millennial community; this, along with his attacks on the pope, would lead to his arrest and execution as a heretic in 1498. While Savonarola's prophecies failed to come to fruition, his attacks on the corruption of the church paved the way for later reform efforts. This included the one led by a German monk named Martin Luther, whose reforming work began two decades after Savonarola's execution.

Martin Luther and the Beginnings of Reformation

Martin Luther, a German monk and biblical scholar, came to believe his church was corrupt and needed reform. This happened after a visit to Rome and his encounter with preachers of indulgences who promised relief from purgatory in exchange for offerings. Luther largely embraced Augustine's spiritualized eschatology, using millennial language to describe the church's history, without expecting Christ's millennial reign on earth. Despite his initial discomfort with the book of Revelation (of which he opined in 1522 that God's "spirit cannot fit itself into this book. There is one sufficient reason for me not to think highly of it—Christ is not taught or known in it"[1]). As time passed, Luther came to see

Revelation as a useful response to the evils of his age, including his conviction that the papacy itself was the seat of the antichrist.

While he was averse to setting a date for the second coming, Luther sensed that the end of the age was close. His belief that the pope was the antichrist fed into this sense of foreboding. While he initially thought Pope Leo X was the antichrist, after Leo's death he concluded that the papacy itself was the antichrist. This view became deeply embedded in Protestant thought. Luther combined his view of the papacy with other elements that he believed signaled the approaching day of the Lord: the emergence of the reform movement in the church, belief that the Jews would soon convert, and the anticipated defeat of the Turks. By the end of the 1520s, Luther had begun to lose faith in this possibility. Nevertheless, he passed on to his theological descendants his belief that the papacy is the antichrist.

Luther's reform efforts began with his response to the issue of indulgences, which were connected to the doctrine of purgatory. Preachers like John Tetzel sold indulgences, which would free the souls of the dead from purgatory. Purgatory, according to Roman Catholic doctrine, is a middle state between death and heaven, where people who aren't ready for heaven get purified, making them worthy of heaven. Luther rejected not only the selling of indulgences but purgatory as well. He offered justification by grace through faith as an answer to indulgences and purgatory. Additionally, Luther and John Calvin taught that all inhabitants of heaven are equal. While Luther believed that the last days were close at hand, he was not ready to pinpoint a day. He did believe, however, that his era would be the decisive moment when the antichrist (the pope) would be defeated.

John Calvin and Divine Sovereignty

Soon after Luther began his reform effort in Germany, Ulrich Zwingli did the same in Switzerland. Despite Zwingli's early embrace of reformation, the second-generation reformer John Calvin proved to be the most important figure of the Reformed tradition. While Calvin, like Luther, believed the papacy was the antichrist, he was less inclined to read into current events signs that the end of the age was looming. He tended to avoid appeals to Daniel and Revelation and setting the date of Jesus' return. While he joined Luther in believing that the Reformation could be a sign that the end of the age was at hand, he tempered this view by stressing God's absolute sovereignty. Rooted in his doctrine of predestination, he assumed the future lies in the sovereign hands of God. Therefore, there's no need to be anxious about the future. As Amy Frykholm writes:

> Calvin's view of the eschatological future was simple: Christ will return. Somehow Christ's reign will be realized on earth. Calvin never commented on Revelation, and he seemed to be suspicious of the millennium's "carnal" leanings. . . . He rejected purgatory as unnecessarily complicated and a cause of corruption in the church. He taught that judgment came immediately at the moment of death, and there was nothing the living could do about the fate of any particular soul, nor really about the fate of their own souls.[2]

For Calvin, salvation is an act of grace, and those whom God chooses to save will enjoy a heavenly future.

Eschatology and the Radical Reformation

While Luther, Zwingli, Calvin, and Thomas Cranmer (England) represent the magisterial reformation, which often partnered with the state and took cautious steps toward reform, others pushed reform in more radical directions. Some of these radical reformers embraced apocalyptic visions. While Luther, Zwingli, and Calvin sought to reform the church they inherited, Anabaptists and other radicals believed these reform efforts didn't go far enough in rooting out corruption and living into the New Testament picture of the church. One of the markers of radical reform was believers' baptism. The term "anabaptist" refers to the act of rebaptism, which had political connotations, since baptism was understood to mark not only one's entrance into the church but also one's citizenship in the state.

One of the leading radical figures was Thomas Müntzer (1489–1525), an early reforming colleague of Luther. Unlike Luther and Calvin, Müntzer rejected the idea of an invisible church composed of wheat and tares, which would be separated on the day of judgment. He not only believed the harvest time Jesus spoke of in Matthew 13:30 had dawned; he believed it was his calling to begin the harvest and initiate the millennial rule. To this end, he embraced the idea of a purified community that shared all things in common. He also embraced the Peasants' Revolt of 1525, which sought to throw off much of the repression heaped on peasants by the upper classes. Müntzer believed this revolt would help fulfill his apocalyptic vision of the end of the age. However, the authorities quashed the revolt, and he was captured and beheaded.

Other apocalyptic preachers followed in Müntzer's wake, with some engaging in violent efforts in pursuit of the millennium. Hans Hut claimed that Jesus would return on Pentecost Sunday in 1528. He proclaimed that the sword would remain sheathed until Christ's return. Then Christ would put the sword in the hands of the saints, who would usher in the kingdom. He died in prison in 1527, before the promised return of Christ could take place, but he wasn't the last apocalyptic preacher. Though some Anabaptists such as Conrad Grebel were pacifists and spoke against violence, apocalyptic episodes continued to take place that tarred the Radical Reformation for generations.

The most notorious efforts occurred in the city of Münster, where followers of Melchior Hoffman, a former Lutheran preacher who claimed to be the prophet Elijah, sought to create the New Jerusalem. Hoffman never visited Münster, but the city became a refuge for radicals. These radicals took control of the city, embraced the community of goods and later practiced polygamy while seeking to launch the millennial kingdom. This experiment ended when political and religious authorities in the region laid siege to the city. When the remnant refused to surrender, they were killed. In the minds of most Europeans, Anabaptism was linked to the excesses of Münster.

It would take the work of figures such as Menno Simons to right the ship and undo the stain of Münster. Simons was originally a priest from the Low Countries before converting to Anabaptism. Once a follower of Melchior Hoffman, like the majority of Anabaptists he came to reject all forms of violence. He assumed that the gathered church would experience persecution until Jesus returned to set up the kingdom of God. As Frederick Baumgartner notes, "by convincing most Anabaptists that suffering persecution by the wicked was a sign of their election, Menno was able to turn them away from violent resistance to the authorities. As a biblical literalist, he emphasized the statement that only God knows the day and hour of the Parousia; the saints must wait patiently for it to occur."[3] Anabaptists, including the Mennonites, have embraced the idea of being a nonconformist, nonviolent peace church.

Puritanism, the English Civil War, and Millennialism

The English and Scottish Reformations of the sixteenth century followed patterns similar to those on the Continent. During the 1530s, Henry VIII began to allow elements of reform to emerge, but reform didn't begin to take hold in England until the reign of his son Edward VI (r. 1547–1553). Because his reign was brief, and his sister Mary I sought to restore Catholicism in England, the cause of reform stalled for a time. Mary's anti-Protestant policies led to the executions of a large number of Protestants, including Thomas Cranmer, the archbishop of Canterbury. John Foxe's *Book of Martyrs* told the stories of these martyrs, becoming one of the most popular books of the day. Although Queen Elizabeth I (r. 1559–1603) took a moderate path in her return to the pathway of reform, preventing an ascendent Puritanism from becoming a political problem during her reign, the same would not be true for her seventeenth-century successors, James I and his son Charles I.

While James was able to navigate the challenges, his son Charles ended up facing a Parliament dominated by Puritans, who would execute him and inaugurate a Puritan commonwealth ultimately dominated by Independents led by Oliver Cromwell. From 1640 to the restoration of the monarchy in 1660, millennialist fervor took hold in England. Many of the Puritans who overthrew the monarchy saw themselves as God's elect facing down the papal antichrist and his ally, whom they identified as the English king. Among these Puritan millennialists were radical factions that included the Levelers, Fifth Monarchy Men, Diggers, and Quakers.

The Levelers were essentially a political movement, though their leader, John Lilbourne, was an Independent (Congregationalist) who believed the second coming was imminent. To prepare for that day, Lilbourne called for the establishment of a just government in England. He also called for men twenty-one and older who owned at least some property to be given equal rights in the nation and the right to elect members to the House of Commons. The Diggers, led by Gerald Winstanley, pushed the call for equality even further. Winstanley claimed to have received visions from the Holy Spirit that led to his advocacy for universal male suffrage. The name, Diggers, reflects their embrace of the community of good, where all members of the community tilled the soil. Frederick Baumgartner writes that Winstanley "argued that humanity lost its innocence when men began to buy and sell property, and thereby create distinctions among men based on wealth. If the land was free for use by all and the world was restored to its 'virgin state' by returning to the communalism and equality of the early Church, it would set the stage for the Parousia."[4]

If the Levelers and Diggers sought to create a more equal society in England, the Fifth Monarchy Men were known for their militancy and became a major force within the New Model Army. Taking their name from the book of Daniel, they believed Charles I fit the image of the tenth king of the fourth evil empire, which Daniel called the "little horn." According to their reading of Daniel 7, with the fall of Charles, the kingdom had been given to the righteous. They would then rule until Jesus returned. Thus, they saw themselves as the vanguard of the rule of the saints, even demanding a Parliament elected from among the saints.

Cromwell initially entertained semitheocratic views of government, which were embodied in the "Barebones Parliament." However, seeing the movement's excesses, he rejected their demands. After Cromwell rejected their demands, the Fifth Monarchy Men declared him to be the beast and tried to overthrow his rule. Although the more radical elements of Puritanism failed to institute a theocracy, they represent a militant version of millennialism that took prophetic passages in Scripture both literally and seriously, assuming they were participating in the last days.

The restoration of the monarch in 1660, along with the reestablishment of an episcopal Church of England, led to great disappointment among adherents of these movements. There would still be millennialist uprisings and movements, but the theocratic and millennialist dreams that led to the overthrow of the monarchy and of the episcopal form of church government were shattered.

While these dreams largely died in England, they remained potent in the American colonies, where Puritanism remained strong. Consider John Winthrop's declaration that the colony in Massachusetts was the "city upon a hill" of Matthew 5:14. These American Puritans sought to create a godly government in the colonies—in essence, a theocracy. They couched their vision in apocalyptic terms. The second coming of Jesus and the establishment of Christ's millennial rule served as sermon fodder for leading preachers such as Cotton Mather. Of course, this effort at establishing a godly realm in the New World also led to the attempted extermination of the indigenous population.

We have traced the story of Christian thinking about the second coming and other millennial expressions, including questions of the afterlife, from the postbiblical era to the early colonization of the Americas. Our journey is not yet complete, but it's time to move into more recent eschatological and apocalyptic expressions.

SECTION THREE

"Are We Going to Be 'Left Behind'?"

The Millennial Voices

Humans often make sense of complicated things by categorizing them. When it comes to the second coming, three terms have emerged that summarize the main ways Christians understand the coming reign of God: premillennialism, postmillennialism, and amillennialism. Many of the ideas behind these terms have old roots.

We begin in chapter 6 by giving attention to premillennialism, which offers one of the best known and most popular contemporary perspectives on the second coming today. In chapter 7 we turn to postmillennialism, which was popular in the nineteenth century and continues to have some influence in North America. Finally, in chapter 8 we explore amillennialism, which in many ways has been the dominant perspective in Western Christianity since Augustine, even though the term itself is relatively modern.

A Key Text: Revelation 20:4–6

Revelation 20:4–6 is the only biblical passage that refers directly to a millennium. However, this one passage has proven central to the way Christians view the future and provides the categories we explore in this section. In this passage of the book of Revelation, John reveals that an angel will lock Satan into an abyss for a thousand years to prevent Satan from troubling the nations (Rev. 20:1–3). John continues:

> I saw thrones on which were seated those who had been given authority to judge. And I saw the souls of those who had been beheaded because of their testimony about Jesus and because of the word of God. They had not worshiped the beast or its image and had not received its mark on their foreheads or their hands. They came to life and reigned with Christ *a thousand years*. (The rest of the dead did not come to life until the thousand years were ended.) This is the first resurrection. Blessed and holy are those who share in the first resurrection. The second death has no power over them, but they will be priests of God and of Christ and will reign with him for *a thousand years*. (Rev. 20:4–6 NIV)

This passage assumes that God raises from the dead the faithful who were identified as martyrs in Revelation 6:9–11. The resurrected martyrs then rule the earth with Jesus for one thousand years. Among the important questions for interpreting the text are:

- Does the text refer to a literal one-thousand-year period when Jesus and the martyred faithful rule? If so, when does that event occur relative to other events that are part of the end times?
- If the text refers not to a literal millennium but uses the language of "a thousand years" in a figurative way, what does the text have in mind when it speaks of the millennium?

As we will see, each of the three millennialisms answers the questions differently. By becoming acquainted with each viewpoint, we'll be better equipped to decide which view makes the most sense to us. Before we get to the three leading perspectives on the millennium, we set the historical context for this conversation.

Postmillennialism and Manifest Destiny in North America

Puritanism found safe harbor in New England, which many Puritans viewed as the New Israel. Therefore, they viewed North America as a sacred place where the Realm of God could be revealed. We see in this the birth of American exceptionalism, the idea that the United States is God's special nation, an exception in its purity and mission.

Postmillennialism is reflected in the message preached during the First Great Awakening (1730s–1770s). Many participants in this awakening hoped to Christianize North America so it could fulfill its calling to be the New Israel. Writing in 1776, Timothy Dwight spoke of the emerging United States serving as an expression of God's light, such that he spoke of two centuries of progress leading up to the year 2000. This vision of God's work in the United States, as the nation moved westward, was expressed in the concept of manifest destiny, the idea that God had planned a great destiny for the United States that was becoming manifest in history. The Second Great Awakening enhanced this millennialist message of progress as it cut across the frontier.

Among those who embraced this vision of progress was Alexander Campbell, one of the founders of the movement known as the Disciples of Christ. Campbell's journal carried the title *Millennial Harbinger.* He envisioned a restored church along the lines of what he called the "Ancient Order of Things," which would lead to Christian unity and a millennial church that would prepare the way for the Realm of God. He envisioned the United States playing a leading part in making this possible. Campbell and other postmillennialists of the day carried with them a sense of optimism about the future of Christianity and its spread across the globe, beginning with the United States.

Return of Premillennialism

While postmillennialism proved attractive to a nation on the move, there was also a premillennialist movement alongside it. This movement was much less optimistic about the future spread of Christianity across the globe. For some, the end was near at hand. Perhaps the most famous of the millennialist expressions of the first half of the nineteenth century was that of William Miller, a Baptist minister. Like many interpreters of apocalyptic literature, Miller scoured Scripture, especially Daniel and Revelation, and calculated the exact moment when Jesus would return. Gathering followers during the 1830s, Miller calculated that Jesus would return in either 1843 or 1844. He narrowed down his date to October 22, 1844, a date he took from his reading of Daniel 8:14 and the fact that it was the date of the Jewish Day of Atonement in that year. He used Daniel's reference to 2,300 days to trace back 2,300 years to the year 458 BCE, when, according to Miller, Artaxerxes I of Persia authorized Ezra to return to Jerusalem and rebuild the temple. When Jesus didn't return in 1843, as he originally expected, Miller came up with the 1844 date. As 1844 faded away, Miller's followers began to drift away, leading to what became known as "the great disappointment." While Miller gave up his preaching of Christ's second coming and died not long afterward in 1849, not everyone gave up on his message.

Among those who continued to hold to the message was Ellen G. White, who suggested that Jesus returned on that date invisibly to cleanse the heavenly temple. Her interpretations gave birth to what became the Seventh-day Adventist Church. And this movement gave birth to what became the Jehovah's Witnesses, both of which have strong apocalyptic theologies. Most of Miller's followers abandoned his movement, but not all gave up. As Paul Boyer points out, however, Miller's lasting legacy "has been seen as the definitive example of the perils of date setting."[1] It also gave a boost to postmillennialism, as the latter seemed a safer route to go.

A more lasting and influential premillennialist movement is linked to the interpretations of the apocalyptic texts by John

Nelson Darby. That movement is known as dispensationalism, premillennialism, and occasionally even Darbyism. Darby was not the first person to devise a dispensationalist reading of Scripture. We find examples of this going back to the second century CE, but Darby's version of dispensationalism has proven to be influential even to this day. That is true even if those persons who embrace his theory do not know his name. Paul Boyer points out, "Darby taught that God has dealt with mankind in a series of epochs, or dispensations—in each of which the means of salvation differed. While Bible prophecy reveals much about past and future dispensations, it is silent on the present one, the Church Age."[2] According to Darby, the next dispensation would begin with the rapture. This would initiate a seven-year period in which the persons left behind would experience a great tribulation, as indicated in Matthew 24:21. When the seven years ended (without true believers being around to witness it), armageddon, the last battle, would begin. Following this battle, the millennium would begin, during which Christ would rule on earth for a thousand years. After this, the final judgment would take place.

The majority of elements in Darby's scheme were not new, but as Boyer notes, "Darby wove these diverse strands into a tight and cohesive system that he buttressed at every point by copious biblical proof texts, then tirelessly promoted through his writings and preaching tours."[3] Unlike interpreters that envisioned England or the United States as the New Israel, Darby connected his end-time scheme with the Jews. Thus, there were two prophetic tracks. One involved the Jews and the other Gentiles.

The key to the scheme was the return of Jews to the Holy Land, where he expected them to rebuild the temple, which in turn would signal that the return of Christ was close at hand. This apocalyptic movement would find a ready audience among American fundamentalists, through prophecy conferences that emerged during the late nineteenth century and through the publication in 1909 of *The Scofield Reference Bible* by Cyrus I. Scofield, who incorporated Darby's interpretations into his annotations. That Bible became a bestseller in the United States. Thus, as Martyn Whittock notes,

"Today, dispensationalism is a global religious phenomenon and dominates prophetic belief, with tens of millions of adherents. And the *Scofield Reference Bible* played a major part in that process."[4] Scofield would influence figures like Hal Lindsey in the 1970s and Tim LaHaye in the 1990s and early 2000s.

While premillennialism gained a foothold in North America during the nineteenth century and continues to have a major presence within certain sectors of evangelical Christianity, postmillennialism has largely died out. In part, the optimism that drove the movement suffered from disappointments including two world wars. Nevertheless, the theological roots of American exceptionalism and manifest destiny remain with us even today, often mixed in with the pessimism of dispensationalism. While not as prominent as it once was, postmillennialism in some form continues to exist to this day.

6

Premillennialism

Jesus Is Coming Soon

Premillennialism is sometimes called dispensationalism, or chiliasm (from a Latin term for "one thousand"). While not everyone will know these specific terms, readers may be familiar with the ideas the terms represent, because these ideas circulate widely in the church and larger culture. Some contemporary Christians may even believe that this is the only possible biblical view of the second coming. Although we speak here of premillennialism, it is not a monolithic movement. There is a diversity of opinion, with interpretive nuances, when it comes to what the future looks like.

Characteristics of Dispensational Premillennialism

According to this view, the Bible reveals that God has divided history into a series of dispensations (periods of history). In each dispensation, God reveals something more. Premillennialists differ as to the number of dispensations, with as few as three (e.g., law, grace, and Realm of God) and as many as eight, though seven is the most common number. In one premillennial perspective, for instance, these ages include: (1) age of innocence (Gen. 1–3); (2) emergence of conscience (Gen. 3–8); (3) development of civil government (including the authority to inflict the death penalty) (Gen. 9–11); (4) promises to the ancestors (Gen. 12–Exod. 19); (5) period of the Law of Moses (Exod. 20–the birth of the church); (6) age of grace (also the age of the church); (7) eternal Realm (Rev. 21–22). In the seven-dispensation model, much current interest focuses on the transition from the sixth to the seventh dispensation, which, adherents believe, is taking place in our moment of history. Of course, as we saw in the previous section, this phenomenon occurred previously in history.

One of the most important things to know about premillennialism is its view of prophecy and the end times. For premillennialism, the Bible contains specific predictions of things that will happen as the present age moves toward its culmination with the return of Jesus and the beginning of a new world. Premillennialists believe that the Bible points to very specific things that will take place in history on the way to the completion of God's purposes.

Premillennialists approach the prophecies of the Bible as envisioning entities and events in history that will come true in real life. For example, premillennial Christians believe that the millennium, the one-thousand-year reign of Jesus and the faithful souls of Revelation 20:4–6, will occur as an actual event in history. Many Christians outside premillennialism believe that the language of Revelation 20:4–6 concerning the millennium is figurative.

Premillennialists search the Bible for prophecies that speak of the end times. They then put together timelines of events that will unfold as the old age winds down and the new one comes to pass. In each generation some premillennialists have thought the end was imminent, interpreting certain current events as fulfilling biblical predictions portending the end of the age. Other premillennialists are more cautious, suggesting that while it's possible to know the general period of history when these things will occur, one cannot know the precise moment.

Both of these groups tend to look at contemporary events for signs that the end of the age is at hand. Still, others follow Jesus' admonition in the Gospel of Mark: "But about that day or hour no one knows, neither the angels in heaven, nor the Son, but only the Father" (Mark 13:32). They may have an interest in signs that the end is near, but they are cautious in putting the date on the calendar.

Dispensationalists tend to have a certain timeline in mind when it comes to anticipating the end. While there is a diversity of belief within this group concerning the expected events and their interpretation, certain elements are commonly found in these presentations, such as the coming of the antichrist (1 John 2:18, 22; 2 Thess. 2:1–4), Daniel's "prophecy of the seven weeks" (Dan. 9:1–27), the "abomination of desolation" (Mark 13:14), the beast and the false prophet (Rev. 12:18–13:18), as well as the first and second deaths and resurrections (Rev. 20:5–6). Of the many events important in premillennialism, several stand out in popular discussion.

- The tribulation (or the great tribulation). The tribulation is a relatively brief period when the suffering of the world will increase. The tribulation will include such things as violence, the breakdown of social order, disease, natural disaster, famine, drought, and floods. Life becomes chaotic with threats and suffering everywhere. Both the human world and the natural world will be greatly affected. The pain of the tribulation will be so intense that people will cry out for it to end. Premillennialists frequently point to the "Olivet discourse" (Matt. 24) as an especially clear prediction of the tribulation. They also call attention to Revelation 7:14, with its reference to those "who have come out of the great tribulation" (NIV). There are differences of opinion as to when this occurs—before the millennium, in the middle, or after the millennium.
- The rapture. This notion comes from a reading of 1 Thessalonians 4:16–17, in which many premillennialists believe that God will resurrect the faithful who have died (v. 16) and gather them with the rest of the faithful who are alive (v. 17), lifting them from the earth so they will be spared the suffering of the tribulation. Premillennialists offer different interpretations of when the rapture will occur. Some see it taking place before the millennium and others afterward. Some believe the

raptured will simply stay in heaven forever after the rapture, while others believe that they will return after the tribulation to be part of the climactic act of Christ establishing the Realm of God finally and forever.

- The second coming of Jesus. When it comes to the second coming, premillennialists offer different timelines, with some versions calling for Jesus to return more than once. For example, Jesus returns to take away those being raptured and returns a second time to establish the eternal Realm of God. Others believe that at Jesus' second coming the rapture and the establishment of the eternal Realm of God are simultaneous events.

- The millennium. The primary text for understanding the millennium is Revelation 20:4–6. God resurrects the faithful martyrs, presumably with physical resurrection bodies. As we have noted, Jesus and this first group of the resurrected faithful rule for a period of a thousand literal years. The destructive effects of the tribulation fade and the world experiences peace for the duration of the millennium. Premillennialists often note that before the millennium, an angel binds Satan. At the end of the millennium, Satan is released for a brief period (Rev. 20:1–6).

- The last judgment. Premillennialists draw on many passages for their picture of the last judgment, one of the most prominent of which is Revelation 20, especially verses 11–15. A second resurrection occurs in which all people who have not been resurrected in the first resurrection are raised. Those who allied themselves with Satan and the Beast are condemned to a lake of fire. Revelation 21–22 indicates that those who have been faithful will dwell in the New Jerusalem, a cosmic universe so changed that it is called the new heaven and the new earth.

- Israel. Premillennialists see Israel and the church as separate entities; the church is not a continuation of Israel but a new community. Nevertheless, they tend to believe that Israel has a special place in the overall divine plan. Thus, God had hoped that Israel would be God's primary agent of blessing the world. While Israel rejected Jesus as its Messiah, God still must keep God's promises, chief among them that God will return Israel to its own land and temple before the end of the age can occur. Many premillennialists believe this promise has already been fulfilled in the establishment of the state of Israel in 1948, the return of Jerusalem to the control of Israel in 1967, and the move of the embassy of the United States from Tel Aviv to Jerusalem in 2018. Now they await the restoration of the temple as a sign that the end is coming even closer.

The most important element in distinguishing the placement of each element on the timeline is the relationship between the rapture, the millennium, and the second coming.

The Afterlife in Premillennialism

Although most premillennialists assume that the faithful will ultimately be assigned a life of blessing, while the unbelievers will experience hell, there are differences of opinion. Some embrace the idea of a final heavenly existence for those who believe in Christ. In heaven, they live a spiritual existence of eternal perfection and unchanging life experience. Thus, there is freedom from sin and death but no possibility for growth as individuals. This is in line with what many Christians have traditionally expected. However, as Craig Blaising notes, other premillennialists expect that the afterlife involves living in the new creation, a regenerated world. In this model, inhabitants experience bodily resurrection and bodily life in much the same way as life is lived in the present, but with the absence of sin and death in a perfect universe.[1] While the average premillennialist may embrace the more traditional view of a heavenly existence, the idea of living in the new creation has gathered a lot of interest among evangelicals.

7

Postmillennialism

Jesus Will Return after We Get Things Right

Postmillennialism was popular in the eighteenth and nineteenth centuries because it offers an optimistic view of human ability. While premillennialism presumes that Christ must return to set up the millennial kingdom, postmillennialism assumes that Christians will establish the millennial kingdom before Jesus returns to bring about the final judgment. Some postmillennial Christians have spoken of "building the Realm of God" in the sense that their efforts will create the Realm of God on earth, after which, Jesus will return. There are not many pure postmillennialists around today. That is in large part due to the harsh realities of the twentieth century, which included two world wars, genocide, and the beginning of the nuclear age. Nevertheless, postmillennialists continue to be with us, albeit often in a more modest form.

Kenneth Gentry defines postmillennialism as the expectation that the proclamation of the gospel of Jesus Christ will

> win the vast majority of human beings to salvation in the present age. Increasing gospel success will gradually produce a time in history before Christ's return in which faith, righteousness, peace, and prosperity will prevail in the affairs of people and nations. After an extensive era of such

conditions the Lord will return visibly, bodily, and in great
glory, ending history with the general resurrection and the
great judgment of all humankind.[1]

You can see in this definition why many postmillennialists have
embraced world mission, in the expectation that Jesus will return
when the world has had the opportunity to hear and respond to
the gospel message. Hopefully, that will lead to a new world of
peace and prosperity. You can see as well why many adherents
of the social gospel movement were also postmillennialist in orientation, as it speaks to the Christian concern for liberation and
justice as expressions of God's Realm.

Although postmillennialists believe this tradition is of ancient
origin, its modern form tends to be rooted in the Reformed tradition (Calvinism), especially Puritanism. As a movement, it is
distinguished by how it sees the relationship of the millennium
to the second coming of Jesus. While some postmillennialists
expect a literal thousand-year period when Jesus and the martyred faithful rule over the world, most postmillennialists interpret the millennium in a nonliteral fashion, such that this refers
to a very long period when elements of the Realm of God have
been at least partially established. Regarding the second coming,
postmillennialists assume Jesus will return *after* the conclusion
of the millennial age. This age will be marked by peace, prosperity, and, in more recent understandings, scientific and technical advancements. Adherents are encouraged to pursue mission
and justice while building schools and hospitals so that the values
of God's Realm can be experienced in the present. Postmillennialism also expressed itself in efforts to bring unity within the
Christian community. Thus the ecumenical movement had its
birth in the movement for world mission in the late nineteenth
and early twentieth centuries.

Postmillennialists believe that Jesus laid the foundations for
the Realm of God through his earthly ministry and preaching,
teaching, and healing. For postmillennialists, the "millennium"
is a long but unspecified period when people try to build the

Realm that has now stretched to two thousand years, and Jesus has yet to return. When Jesus ascended to heaven, Jesus empowered the church with the Holy Spirit to continue his work of manifesting the qualities of the Realm of God. For most postmillennialists who interpret the biblical reference to the millennium as a symbol for an extended period, the millennium began with the coming of the Spirit. We are living in the millennial age now, and it will conclude with the second coming of Jesus. At the time of the second coming, we will also see the general resurrection, the final judgment, and the complete and eternal disclosure of the Realm of God.

Postmillennialism assumed that people would respond to the empowering presence of the Spirit by converting people and creating disciples who in turn would re-create the social world according to the desires of God. Postmillennialists saw themselves and others reshaping the world along the lines of the Realm of God.

The various liberation theologies that we discuss in chapter 11 tend not to use millennial language or categories. They also don't place a great emphasis on the second coming (though some liberation theologies do include belief in a second coming). Nevertheless, liberation theologies share two characteristics with postmillennialism. First, liberation theologies seek to create a world that is quite similar to one envisioned as the millennium—a world of prosperity, opportunity, freedom, dignity, and access to the material goods necessary for a safe and secure life. Secondly, liberation theologies, like postmillennialism, place great emphasis on human agency in bringing about the liberated world. We see this vision present in Gustavo Gutiérrez's *A Theology of Liberation*: "Without liberating historical events, there would be no growth of the Kingdom. But the process of liberation will not have conquered the very roots of oppression and the exploitation of man by man without the coming of the Kingdom, which is above all a gift."[2] Liberation theologians, like postmillennialists, believe that the Spirit is at work in the world for liberation and that their mission is to identify where the Spirit is trying to bring about liberation and to join that work.

Over the last two generations, a new postmillennialist movement has appeared: Christian reconstructionism (also known as
"Dominion Theology"). Christian reconstructionism seeks to
reconstruct the entire social world according to its interpretation
of divine law. They seek to assert dominion over the world mod-
eled on their interpretation of the Bible and Christian theology.
Christian reconstructionists believe that the Realm of God was
established at the resurrection and that human beings are to submit to the laws of the Bible (from both Testaments) and to exercise dominion in home, church, and government. In their view,
the millennium will commence as the faithful engage in recon-
structing the world according to their view of the Bible. As for
the return of Christ, that will take place when biblical values are
established throughout the world. They believe that this process
may take a very long time—perhaps multiple generations.

While Christian reconstructionists expect a second coming,
they do not dwell on the timing of the last things; they believe that
they have a mandate from God to re-create the culture along the
following lines: The culture is to be theonomous, that is, it is to be
ruled according to the laws of God. (The word "theonomous" is
comprised of two Greek roots: "God" [*theos*] and "law" [*nomos*].)
Christian reconstructionists seek to make biblical laws (including many Old Testament laws) the law of the land. In its extreme
form, Christian reconstructionists have been known to advocate
the death penalty for murder, idolatry, adultery, witchcraft, blas-
phemy, and same-sex relationships. Because of the centrality of
education in forming believers, Christian reconstructionists were
among the first to promote homeschooling. Reconstructionism
accepts only those forms of diversity that are consistent with its
interpretations of biblical principles.

One of the leading exponents of this movement, R. J. Rushdoony, says that the person who is "being progressively sanctified
will inescapably sanctify . . . home, school, politics, economics,
science, and all things else by understanding and interpreting
all things in terms of the word of God."[3] Christian reconstructionists thus seek to bring the society's educational, legal, and

political structures into conformity with their interpretation of biblical principles. In so doing, they see themselves as a conquering force against all that is opposed to the ways of God. Christian reconstructionism sees its work of reconstruction as essential to establishing the Realm of God. While not all Christian nationalists are postmillennialists or reconstructionists, this philosophy has permeated that movement.

Whatever the expression of this perspective, the focus is not so much on a literal millennium, but on the expectation that God's Realm will be experienced in this earthly context. The message of postmillennialism is that God's Realm will eventually encompass the earth, to the glory of God.

8

Amillennialism

Jesus Is Already Here in the Church

In its simplest forms, amillennialism is attractive to many Christians. It puts forward the hope of a second coming when God will make all things right, while not tying that hope to a complicated end-time scenario. In fact, in its basic manifestation, many of the ideas of amillennialism are similar to those of the open-ended expectation of the timing of the second coming that we saw as the main way of thinking in the Western church since at least Augustine in the fourth century CE, or perhaps earlier with Origen in the third century CE. Thinking of more contemporary connections, amillennialist perspectives also have certain similarities to the "already . . . not yet" or partially realized interpretations of the Realm of God that we take up in chapter 10.

The term "amillennial" is of recent vintage, though the core philosophy goes back to the New Testament period. The word as we have it today has been used to differentiate its adherents from premillennialists and postmillennialists. The term "amillennial" designates a theology that denies the existence of a historical millennium. That is, whatever the millennium refers to in Revelation 20, it is not a literal time period. The basic theme of amillennialism is an open-ended expectation of the second coming, without a literal thousand-year period during which Christ will reign with the saints before the day of judgment. Most amillennialists read biblical prophecy nonliterally.

For amillennialists, when Jesus appeared for the first time, he launched significant aspects of the Realm of God; but he has yet to return to complete the final and full manifestation of the Realm. Using dispensational language, the reign of Jesus has already taken root in the age of the church (or the age of grace). People experience this Realm spiritually as they await its climactic completion after the second coming. Accordingly, millennial language is figurative. Many use the term more broadly as a symbol for the reign of God already taking place on earth in a spiritual way but with the expectation that something more must happen: Christ must return and complete the work of redemption. Few amillennialists expect a complicated set of end-time developments as they await Jesus' return. However, amillennialists are diverse in the precise ways they understand the nature of what happens during the period they symbolically name the millennium.

Many amillennialists think of the millennium in terms of an inner experience of Christ's sovereignty and the quality of fellowship in the church. While human beings are on earth, they experience the Realm of God in spiritual ways. Such a believer might say, "I feel the Realm of God in my heart." The spirituality of the Realm in the heart can be manifest in relationships in the church and the values and practices of the larger world. Amillennialists do not believe their work can bring in the final and complete state of the Realm, but they do believe they can foreshadow many of its qualities in the present.

The spiritual millennium is a temporary—if prolonged—experience of the rule of Christ and the faithful in the circumstances of the present. But the final and full experience of the Realm awaits a literal second coming. At that time, Jesus will carry out the final judgment and then put in place his own permanent rule, as he reigns with the faithful in the new heaven and the new earth. When this time comes, God's ultimate purposes will find their completion both physically and spiritually. This is forever.

A good many Christians embrace amillennialism. They regard this viewpoint as consistent with their interpretation of the Bible and God's ultimate purposes. In particular, amillennialism allows for an "already . . . not yet" view of Christ's rule. Amillennialists find this view present in Scripture, such as when Paul says, "For now we see in a mirror, dimly, but then we will see face to face. Now I know only in part; then I will know fully, even as I have been fully known" (1 Cor. 13:12). Amillennialism provides a vocabulary and theological categories that enable adherents to distinguish themselves from premillennialists and postmillennialists. Amillennialism allows them to focus on the fundamentals of Christian life and witness without being distracted by questions about when the last things will occur.

SECTION FOUR

"How Do We Make Sense of the Second Coming Today?"

Contemporary Voices

A s we turn to voices in the contemporary world, we need to keep in mind that people continue to subscribe to viewpoints from the past. Views from the past include the three millennialist forms we have just discussed as well as other viewpoints from the past, though contemporary Christians often update those perspectives to account for current realities and expectations.

In chapters 9 through 13, we survey several viewpoints that emerged in the twentieth century and remain popular in the first decades of the twenty-first century. These aren't the only current or emergent forms of eschatological thinking, but they're representative, and we hope they will spark conversation about the way we envision the future.[1]

In each case, Christians drew on earlier perspectives, including apocalyptic thinking in the New Testament, as they developed responses to questions and issues emerging in the contemporary world. As we explore each of these interpretations, we bring into the conversation two overarching themes.

1. What can we make of the fact that the apocalyptic understanding of the second coming has not occurred in the way or in the time frame anticipated by the New Testament writers (or many writers since that time)?
2. What can the church say and do about the fact that since the time of the first century CE injustice and suffering continue? The second coming promises a remade world, yet the same old world keeps going on.

Before turning to the viewpoints, we note that while few Christians today use the language of postmillennialism, there is quite a bit of similarity between several of these perspectives and an important aspect of postmillennialism. Like postmillennialism, some of these perspectives emphasize the importance of human activity in the present as the agency to bring about God's purposes.

In chapter 13 we turn to the Orthodox tradition, which manifests great continuity with its original impulses, while also responding to what the Orthodox perceive as a deepening awareness of the relationship of God with the world.

9

Separating the Core from the Container

Demythologizing the Second Coming

A reader may be surprised to find the expression "separating the core from the container" as a designation for a way of interpreting the biblical expectation that Jesus will return. This way of speaking derives from differences between the worldview of the Bible and the scientific worldview that emerged from the Enlightenment (mid-1700s to early 1800s). As explained in the chapter that follows, we offer this way of speaking because it captures the essence of demythologizing, in which the interpreter separates the worldview in which the second coming is cast (the container) from the core meaning. A more vivid way of saying the same thing is to speak of separating the husk of an ear of corn from the kernels on the cob within. The husk contains the corn, but the husk is not essential to the ear of corn itself.

At the time the biblical materials were written, most people believed that the universe was relatively small and that the earth was its center. They believed the universe itself was like a three-story house. The upper story was heaven, where God and the angels dwelled. God controlled the universe from heaven and occasionally sent messages and messengers to earth. The middle story was the earth, with its mountains, plains, oceans, cities, and people. On the one hand, people had considerable freedom in the exercise of their lives. On the other hand, God had extensive power and could intervene in the life of the created world. God or an agent of God could come down from heaven to speak and act on the earth. The lower story was the basement. At different times people believed different things about what was in the basement, ranging from a great primeval sea to a place of punishment (hell).

In a three-story universe, it made sense to think of Jesus ascending to heaven after the resurrection and later returning to earth to complete the work of bringing the Realm of God into being. One could speak of "heaven above" and "things below" in a direct and physical way. However, with the Enlightenment and the coming of the scientific worldview, many people began to think of the universe in more complicated ways. They saw the earth no longer as the center of the universe but as one planet in a vast space that had many other planets. Many scientists have come to think of the universe as ever expanding.

From the scientific point of view, it no longer made sense to speak literally of heaven above, the earth in the middle, and the underworld below. If we say Jesus ascended after the resurrection, where did he go? In an ever-expanding universe, is there really a designated area we might call heaven? If there is no such place, how can we think of Jesus coming a second time in the way described in the Bible? Similar questions can be asked of many other biblical materials, because many biblical passages assume the three-story universe and God (or God's agents) coming down to influence things on earth in direct and physical ways.

However, Rudolf Bultmann, a German thinker who raises such questions, says, "It is impossible to repristinate a past world picture by sheer resolve, especially a mythical world picture now that all of our thinking is irrevocably formed by science. A blind acceptance of New Testament mythology would be simply arbitrariness; to make such acceptance a demand of faith would be to reduce faith to a work."[1] Faced with such questions and issues, Bultmann sought a way to bridge the world of the Bible and the scientific consciousness. He wanted the Christian faith to be believable to people who accept a scientific worldview. He wanted to preserve the best of ancient tradition while making it compatible with contemporary reason. Many Christians joined him.

Bultmann introduced a way of interpreting the Bible called demythologizing. Bultmann noticed that the language of the Bible and the language of science are two different ways of speaking about the world. The language of science is clear and factual. It tries to describe things as they are in a one-to-one fashion. By contrast, much of the language of the Bible is poetic, figurative, and evocative. Indeed, Bultmann and many others use the word "myth" to describe much of the Bible. Myth doesn't refer to something untrue. Instead, Bultmann notes that in the ancient world, people spoke in mythic language to describe how they experienced the world. In figurative stories, they described how they felt about life. They would articulate their understanding of life through the setting, characters, and plot of a mythic story.

Bultmann and others take the view that human experience in the ancient and contemporary worlds is similar. The ancient and contemporary cultural forms in which these experiences come to life may be different. People today use different language to speak about these feelings than they did in antiquity. But the underlying insight is the functional equivalent. A biblical passage may put forward a significant theological meaning not dependent on the scientific factuality of the statement. Today's people taking Bultmann seriously try to describe the core significance of the passage in today's terms.

Such Christians believe that the biblical texts pointing to the second coming are mythological. People in the biblical periods experienced the world as a place of sin, idolatry, pride, inauthenticity, injustice, falsehood, slavery, and violence. They used the language of the three-story (mythological) worldview to speak of their experience of recognizing that these things did not have the final and determining word for them. When they believed in Jesus and his return, they experienced release from the old false existence and discovered the freedom that comes from forgiveness, recognition of the living God as the creator and sustainer, humility that leads to community, and other upbuilding qualities of life that come from believing in God.

The core meaning of the second coming is not that Jesus will arrive on the clouds, but that God provides redemption from being trapped by characteristics of life associated with the old age. Believing that God provides this release provides the believer with the functional equivalent of the experience of the second coming. In a sense, in the figurative language of antiquity, the second coming happens in the present again, and again, and again.

We return to the container and the core as an image for this approach to the second coming. The outer container is the mythological story, the biblical images of Jesus returning from heaven on the clouds in glory, accompanied by the angels. The deeper meaning is the core, that is, the idea that people in the present are freed to live authentically for God and themselves when they have faith. This approach is a form of the realized Realm (realized eschatology) we have mentioned previously. The experience of release and empowerment in the present is the functional equivalent of the release and empowerment that the ancients believed would result from the second coming.

Christians who take the approach of husking the mythic picture of the second coming do not expect a cosmic event that will end one age and begin another. The preaching and teaching of the deep meaning of the second coming offer people a choice: to believe or to reject that God offers them the possibility of release from the present and the ability to live freely and authentically in the present and the future. The second coming is not an event in the future but is possible at any and every moment.

For this group, the effect of the story of the second coming does not take place because God initiates a change in history. The effects of the mythical event of the second coming come about as human beings receive the possibility of renewed life. When we decide to trust God, we experience forgiveness, release, and empowerment to live fully and courageously in the present.

It is important to realize that those who promote this perspective do so in order to show that the Christian faith can be intellectually credible today. One of our friends refers to this phenomenon as a salvage operation: the church seeks to salvage teachings from texts with a mythic overlay by casting those teachings in ways that people today can accept. Indeed, the effort to husk the corn and expose the ear has an evangelistic quality. It seeks to offer moderns a way to turn away from idols, sin, and falsehood and to receive renewal from a living God.

10

The Presence of the Future

The Theology of Hope

What does the future have to do with the present? Even if the reign of God has not come in its fullness, does that mean it is not yet present in some form? People put questions such as these to apocalypticism. These are serious questions, because, in the words of the late German New Testament scholar Ernst Käsemann, apocalypticism is "the mother of all Christian theology." He writes that "the coming of the kingdom of God is already manifest on earth where the Nazarene appears and is accepted." In that vein, when it comes to the end of the world, "according to the New Testament and its apocalyptic, the end of the world begins with the appearance of the one on whom the heavens opened, on whom the Spirit descended, and of whom it was announced, 'My Son, the Beloved.'"[1] That is, apocalypticism is the foundation for the way we understand the Christian faith.

Among those who embraced an apocalyptic vision of Christian theology but modified it for the contemporary world is Käsemann's former student Jürgen Moltmann. Moltmann and others like him, beginning in the 1960s, sought to envision a new future for the world that invites Christians to commit themselves to live into the promise of the Realm of God. In his first major work, he laid out his vision of a *Theology of Hope*. In this foundational work, Moltmann defined hope christologically. In his view, the resurrection of Jesus serves as an answer to the cross, so that the future can begin to take shape in the present. Moltmann began to think of apocalyptic hope in terms of the "already . . . not yet."

When Moltmann began to lay out his eschatological vision, the world found itself in a period of great uncertainty about the future. World War II ended with the inauguration of the atomic age, which promised the possibility of mutually assured destruction. Moltmann sought to offer hope for the future, but without the millenarianism that he believed had "mobilized Europe's various seizures of power over the world and gave them their orientation" that they could be a master race ruling the world. This form of manifest destiny, he suggests, is rooted in the expectation that when Christ returns the saints will reign with him for a thousand years, making this the last empire.[2] Moltmann offered a different view of the future than the one encapsulated in this millenarian vision.

Moltmann's theological vision is thoroughly centered in the future, wherein we can move toward Christ's reign not in a future world but in this world. Therefore, this "Christianity is wholly and entirely confident hope, a stretching out to what is ahead, and a readiness for a fresh start." The future is "the essential element of the faith." As such, it is Easter faith, for "faith means living in the presence of the risen Christ and stretching out to the coming kingdom of God."[3]

Moltmann's eschatology, his view of last things, is rooted in the "coming of God." That is, he teaches that God is coming to us, from the future. "The coming of God means the coming of a being that no longer dies and a time that no longer passes away. What comes is eternal life and eternal time."[4] While Moltmann embraces an eschatological theology, it is not millenarian. That is, he does not envision either armageddon or a literal millennium as the future, but he recognizes that the future is yet to be determined. Since we do not know how much time is left for the earth, "we must act today as if the future of all humankind depended on us, and yet at the same time trust that God will remain loyal to God's own creation, and will not let it fall."[5]

Moltmann's view of the future is rooted in his doctrine of the Trinity, which is thoroughly relational. For him, the Trinity is comprised of three divine subjects existing in a mutually loving relationship. This relationship within the Trinity is foundational to God's relationship with the world. It is here that the church figures in his eschatology. As Richard Bauckham notes, the church's existence is rooted in the mission of the Son and the Spirit, such that "by participating in these missions, the church has the messianic role of being a provisional anticipation of the coming universal kingdom of God."[6] For Moltmann, God's goal is the healing and salvation of the entire cosmos. This is his eschatological vision—the presence of God's rule of earth. We can experience this rule in part in the present, but fully only after God remakes the world.

In Moltmann's view, the "heart of the Christian message" is rooted in God's victory over death in the resurrection of Jesus. Therefore, he writes that "where Christ is present there is life and there is hope in the struggle of life against the powers of death."[7]

When it comes to divine judgment, the idea that Christ will mete out retributive justice on humanity is contrary to the message of Jesus of Nazareth. Believing that God judges in wrath, he acknowledges, has not only done great spiritual and psychological damage, but has been rejected by a great many. Instead of believing that God is our judge, our tendency is to view humans as being responsible for our ultimate destiny. Heaven or hell is, thus, our choice.

Moltmann finds this wanting and so offers a different vision, a vision of God's justice acting on behalf of those who are powerless and suffering. God is the one who judges and makes things right. He writes that "as the coming judge of the victims and perpetrators of sin, the risen Christ will bear the suffering of the one and the burden of the other, so as to bring both out of the rule of darkness into the light of God's kingdom."[8] In other words, divine judgment serves to makes things right, to achieve reconciliation. That is because "all the disrupted conditions in creation must be put right so that the new creation can stand on the firm ground of righteousness and justice, and can endure to eternity."[9] As for whether this suggests universal salvation, the answer is rooted in a "cosmic Christology, according to which 'death will be destroyed' (1 Cor. 15:26) and hell annihilated."[10]

But before that day comes, we live out the presence of the future in the present moment as we look to the future, so that as we put our trust in God's coming, "we open ourselves for his life-giving Spirit, and experience the healing and liberating forces of that Spirit." These are not miraculous powers, but these powers of the age to come "come out of the promised future of Christ into our present and fill us with new vitality."[11] Thus, we can participate in the work of God to bring in the present signs of God's Realm. So, as the people of God, filled with the Spirit, we push against that which is contrary to God's Realm and promote that which is rooted in God's reign. So "we shall, already, here and now, let something of the healing and new creation of all things be seen which we expect in the future."[12]

The hope that is rooted in God's future is present with us now, as we embody God's Realm. That future includes some form of eternal life. That moment of resurrection for us, according to Moltmann, takes place on the day of our death. He writes: "Our hour of death is the hour of our resurrection. When we die, we wake to eternal life. The pains of death are the birth pains into eternal life. While our body with the 'sum' of its limbs lies dead and decays, the entirety of our life, the 'whole' of our living soul, will rise again with a new body to everlasting life."[13]

11

Creating a Just World Now and in the Future

Liberation Theology

Liberation theology is a distinctive theological movement whose advocates are found in many Christian denominations and movements today. The origins of liberation theology can be found in Latin America during the late 1960s and early 1970s, though its roots go back much further. There is a wide variety of liberationist movements in the world today. While we look to Latin America as the starting point, Black liberation theology emerged about the same time. Over time movements emerged among other groups and communities. Thus there is feminist liberation theology (primarily white women), Womanist theology (African American women), as well as the Mujerista movement (Latina women). There is Minjung theology that is Korean in origin, as well as Dalit theology that originated in India. There is also queer theology and disability theology. Each of these movements is rooted in the Christian faith and committed to the liberation of those people who experience oppression in some form. While sharing some common themes, each expression of liberation theology has nuances that are connected to its immediate context.

Broadly speaking, liberation theology offers a message of salvation that is focused on the transformation of the world in which oppression occurs. Miguel De La Torre points out that while the "common starting point of theological reflection is the existential experience of the marginalized, the ultimate goal remains liberation from the reality of societal misery."[1] The most common forms of repression that liberationists seek to overcome are related to race, ethnicity, gender, sexual orientation, economic exploitation, national origin, physical disability, and religion. Some liberation theologians also call attention to God's desire to liberate the natural world from human abuse.

How this takes place depends on the situation in which people find themselves. As for the nature of God's Realm, liberation theologians believe that it is already breaking into the present, even if its ultimate fulfillment takes place in the future. Therefore, the focus of the people of God is on pursuing social transformation that comes about as God works through human agency to bring into the present the values and practices of the Realm of God. As one of the early liberation theologians, Gustavo Gutiérrez, noted, justice requires confidence in the future: "The commitment to the creation of a just society and, ultimately, to a new man, presupposes confidence in the future. This commitment is an act open to whatever comes."[2]

This school of thought insists that justice is a primary value of the Realm of God. Consequently, they believe God desires that justice become present in human history. By justice, liberation theology means a social world in which all people are treated with dignity and respect, live together in peace and mutual support, have access to the necessary material resources for a full and secure life, and have the freedom to pursue their full potential as human beings. These resources include not only life basics— such as food, clothing, and housing—but also adequate financial resources, meaningful employment, education, health care, and other things that make for a life whose characteristics are similar to those of life in the Realm of God.

Liberation theologians contend that the Christian religion, by the way the church talks about life after death and the second coming of Jesus, has often numbed people to their oppression and the possibilities of liberation from that oppression. Indeed, Karl Marx claimed that religion is the opiate of the people, because it uses the promise of heaven to deaden the pain of this life and therefore make the poor and marginalized more compliant to those in power. Religion encourages a person to think, "If I can just endure the conditions of the present, I will be rewarded in the future." This view can easily lead to human passivity in the face of repression. In contrast to that message, liberationists envision Jesus being the liberator. Jesus is understood to dwell among us, sharing in the poverty and oppression experienced by the marginalized in society. Thus, the cross is not necessarily the means of atonement but a sign of solidarity with those who experience crucifixion today.

Because liberation theology teaches that God is at work seeking to transform society so that the values of God's Realm are present in the here and now, it encourages and empowers people to become agents of social transformation. Thus, it is concerned with the whole human being and with human communities in all their dimensions—social, political, economic, and religious. Liberation proponents seek to confront all attitudes and behaviors that undermine justice in communities, such as racism, sexism, colonialism, homophobia, economic exploitation, and authoritarianism in government and other forms of human community.

Liberationists emphasize that these oppressive realities are not simply matters of prejudice or exertion of power on the part of individuals but are systems that are bigger than any individual. Racism, for instance, is the combination of prejudice with the power to use that prejudice to repress and exploit others. Racism is an attitude of prejudice in white communities that is transmitted in the values of the communities and manifests itself in denying dignity, opportunity, freedom, and even life itself to people of color. Prophets of liberation hope not only to see liberating change take place in the attitudes and behaviors of individuals but also to see the transformation of systems.

As noted above, liberation theology is rooted in the belief that Jesus is the liberator whose preaching inaugurated the Realm of God. While the crucifixion was an act of solidarity with the oppressed, the resurrection of Jesus is the first fruit of the Realm. But the resurrection is only the beginning, not the end of the journey. In making this claim, liberation theology envisions the Realm as not just a religious entity, but also a social and political one. As Jon Sobrino writes concerning Jesus' message:

> Though he proclaimed it for religious reasons, its content is still political, not in opposition to the religious dimension, but for differential from the purely transcendent or individual dimension. The religious and political dimensions have no reason to be mutually exclusive, whether they are seen as different aspects of human existence, or still more, if they are taken on different levels: that of subjective motivation and that of objective motivation.[3]

For liberation theology, the Realm of God is not an abstract concept or simply a spiritual reality. It is often rooted in deep spirituality, but that spirituality leads them to engage in social and political efforts designed to bring about change in society. Liberation thinkers fervently believe that the Realm of God has political dimensions, because it calls for the reorganization of the entire social world so that it provides security, dignity, freedom, opportunity, and abundance for all. Liberation activists often partner with nonreligious individuals and organizations to further the cause of liberation.

Liberation thinkers seldom speak directly about the second coming as a distinct event. They also don't give much attention to the idea that the Realm of God involves a dramatic interruption of history. Indeed, there are some similarities between the vision of liberation theology and postmillennialism, in that they imply that human work for justice is how history will lead to the Realm of God.

If eschatology is, in many ways, a theology of history, a way of understanding the progress of humanity in relationship to God, then God is not liberating people *from* history but liberating them *within* history. As José Míguez Bonino wrote: "The Kingdom is not the denial of history but the elimination of its corruptibility, its frustrations, weakness, ambiguity—more deeply, its sin—in order to bring full realization of the true meaning of the communal life of man."[4] In essence, history is, as Míguez Bonino notes, not a riddle to be solved, but "a mission to be fulfilled." That mission is to be accomplished not in the next life, but in human history. Thus, Christians are called to participate in this work of liberation.

While liberation theologians are focused on the needs of the present, they also are concerned about the future. As James Cone, a pioneer in Black liberation theology, writes: "Jesus Christ is who he will be. He is not only the crucified and risen One but also the Lord of the future who is coming again to fully consummate the liberation already happening in the present."[5] This conviction provides hope in the present that the oppression experienced by the poor and the marginalized will be overcome.

As Cone makes clear, unless this work of theology is done in conversation with those who are poor, oppressed, and marginalized, it will not fully express the message of Jesus. "Thus, when connected with the person of Jesus, hope is not an intellectual idea; rather, it is the praxis of freedom in the oppressed community. To hope in Jesus is to see the vision of his coming presence, and thus one is required by hope itself to live as if the vision is already realized in the present."[6] Martin Luther King Jr., paraphrasing the nineteenth-century transcendentalist leader Theodore Parker, could famously say that "the arc of the moral universe is long, but it bends toward justice." As liberationists remind us, that arc is still bending and has yet to reach completion. It will not reach completion if we do not participate in this work of liberation that points us to the future. But that work of liberation does not fall on the people alone, for God has taken the lead and stands with and for those who are poor and oppressed.

The possibility of the Realm serves as a call to action to transform this world so that justice can be experienced in the present. Therefore, the people of God are called to engage in this work of liberation, as partners with God, to bring into reality that which does not yet exist in its fullness. As José Míguez Bonino puts it, "an eschatological faith makes it possible for the Christian to invest his life historically in the building of a temporary and imperfect order with the certainty that neither he nor his effort is meaningless or lost." He speaks of the confession of belief in the resurrection and life everlasting as being "not a self-centered clinging to one's own life or a compensation for the sufferings of life or a projection of unfulfilled dreams but the confident affirmation of the triumph of God's love and solidarity with [humanity], the witness to the enduring quality of [human] responsible stewardship of creation and of [humankind's] participation in love, the final justification of all fight against evil and destruction."[7]

12

Open-Ended Futures

Open Theism and Process Theology

An important contributor to the conversation about last things is Open and Relational Theology. This approach to the fulfillment of God's purposes takes different forms, but for our initial purposes, we speak of two expressions: open theism and process theology. They share some elements but differ in other ways. Both schools of thought reformulate aspects of traditional Christian teaching. To understand their perspectives on the second coming, we should recognize how they think about God and the world. Hence, we summarize the main lines of each approach and point out similarities and differences.

Much traditional Christian thinking assumes versions of the following.

- God is all-powerful. All things happen in the world either at God's direct initiative or by God's permission. God can intervene in history at any moment. However, God can decide to limit the exercise of God's power. In the latter instance, God is like the parent who could spank the child but who decides not to do so.
- God is all-knowing. God knows everything that happens everywhere in the world, including in the deepest recesses of

the human heart. Many Christians believe that God has specific knowledge of the future, including the choices each person will make before we make them. Other Christians modify this viewpoint, holding that God has a general knowledge of the future while allowing human beings and other elements of creation to make decisions.

- God does not change. Some Christians believe that God's unchangeability means that God has planned a future that cannot change. Other Christians believe that God's nature does not change but that God can change God's decisions. For example, repentance from sin could prompt God to change God's decision from condemning a person or community to saving that person or community.

- God is all-loving. Love is less a feeling and more a decision to act for the good of the other and the community. God always acts for the good.

- God is completely just. We can count on God to do what God says. Some Christians think that the justice of God calls for God to punish the disobedient.

On the one hand, this traditional perspective offers security. Everything is ultimately under God's control. Even when life turns to chaos, people can believe God has control of the chaos. On the other hand, this outlook makes God responsible not only for the good but also for the bad.

The suffering of the innocent raises the biggest question here. If God is all-powerful, altogether loving, and altogether fair, then how can God cause or allow the innocent to suffer? Free will is another important issue. If God is all-powerful and all-knowing, then what is the point of human decisions? Is free will just a charade?

For many traditional Christians, the second coming brings about the final judgment and the beginning of the new age, and thus resolves all questions about the power, love, and justice of God. God does what is right for all. God rewards the obedient and punishes the disobedient. Human beings, with our limited perception, cannot grasp God's reasons for why things happen.

As someone in a Bible study said, "The ways of God are mysterious. We cannot understand them, but we must accept them."

Open Theism

Open theism is a broad category for Christians who agree that the future is open. For open theists, God limits God's exercise of power in the present. God thus opens the door for the exercise of free will. While God may ultimately be powerful, God chooses to act noncoercively in the present. There are some things God will not do, because God has limited God's own exercise of power. Regarding God's knowledge, open theists agree that God knows all that there is to know, but since much of the future depends on human choices and actions, God cannot know completely what that future will look like until God decides to wrap up history.

For open theists, human beings (and other elements of nature) are endowed with free will. Therefore, God does not plan specific circumstances for individuals, households, or groups. People and other inhabitants of creation create their own lives through the choices they make. Through the Bible, Christian tradition, and other resources, God offers people guidance on how to live in ways that are loving and just, but God chooses not to force this advice on the human family. Human choices in response to God's guidance determine the immediate future. God has not planned the future in detail. That is why this viewpoint is called *open* theism: the future is truly open.

When it comes to the second coming of Jesus and the matter of God fulfilling God's ultimate promises, open theists are diverse. Though they believe that God could send Jesus for a single dramatic apocalyptic event, few open theists believe God will take this route, because it would deny human freedom. While God will fulfill God's purposes, most open theists believe that neither we nor God can know just how this will occur, since it depends on the joint participation of God and the human family. Open theists think, "Yes, we believe a final fulfillment will occur, but we cannot know when or how."

Open theists believe that some form of an afterlife exists. Included in the afterlife is the assumption that, as found in Scripture, humans will face divine judgment. For the most part, open theists reject universal salvation, because that assumes God can and does overrule human freedom. A typical open-theist position is that the decisions that we make in this life follow us into the next one. Thus, God does not consign human beings to hell, but our choices may create for ourselves a desolate afterlife. Here, however, the future is still open. Thomas Jay Oord, a leading open theist, speaks of God's unrelenting love pursuing human beings into the afterlife. "God everlastingly invites creatures to relationships of love in this life and the next." However, because God, out of love, grants us freedom, we can reject this invitation. "When we do, we suffer the *natural* negative consequences that come from saying no to the positive power of love." Nevertheless, Oord can envision the possibility that in the end, all will cooperate with God.[1] What remains undefined is how this ultimately works, especially after death.

Some Christians are attracted to the open theist perspective because it preserves the security associated with the traditional view: God will find a way to fulfill God's purposes. At the same time, it offers human beings a meaningful view of freedom. Human choices make real differences in the present and the future.

Process (Relational) Theology

Process theology is sometimes called relational theology. This thinking has its origins in the first half of the twentieth century through the writings of the English philosopher Alfred North Whitehead and the North American philosopher Charles Hartshorne. The word "process" is key to understanding this movement. It assumes that all elements of existence are constantly in process, that is, they are constantly experiencing movement or change. God too changes in one way though not in another. Process theology sees God as being di-polar, that is, having two central agencies that work completely with one another. One aspect of God continues forever: God's desire for all elements of creation to live together in inclusive well-being, that is, in communities of mutual support marked by love, peace, justice, and abundance for all. However, God adapts how God expresses God's desire for these things in accord with the actual circumstance of life. God always seeks the optimum expression of love, but from circumstance to circumstance, that love can be manifest in different ways.

As in open theism, human beings and nature create the present and the future through the choices they make. Process theology differs from open theism in one key respect. Process theologians more explicitly believe that God's power *is limited by God's own nature* and not simply because God chooses to relinquish that power. The God of process thought exercises power, not through muscular coercion but through lures or invitations. God invites human communities toward choices that will optimize love, peace, justice, and abundance.

People as individuals and communities can cooperate with God—they can accept God's invitation—or they can choose against the possibilities that God offers and, hence, create a world with less love, peace, justice, and abundance for all. God cannot intervene to change the result of those choices. Human choices limit the possibilities for existence available in a given moment. However, God continually offers fresh possibilities that can lead to the level of inclusive well-being available in a given set of circumstances.

Process theologians do not believe that the second coming can occur as described in the Bible. We no longer think of the world as a three-story universe. More importantly, God does not have the power to replace the present world in a single stroke. However, forms of life will continue until the time when they fundamentally change. For example, the sun will eventually go out. In the new period of existence, God will be constantly present, as God is now, offering possibilities for the peak experience of love available in each moment for the life forms that are present in the changing world. God will invite the elements of the new life forms toward forms of mutual support that are appropriate for those forms.

Process theologians are divided on the question of whether people experience an afterlife. Some process thinkers simply say, "No." They think that when we die, we lose consciousness. As a friend says, "The lights of the mind turn off and never turn on again." Other process theologians, however, believe that at death, the consciousness of the human being does live on as a living consciousness in the mind of God. We no longer have a body. But our awareness—which is a nonmaterial phenomenon—passes into the living consciousness of God, where we continue to be aware of God and others in the perfect love that is the essential nature of God.

One of the major differences in the approach to theology itself between open theism and process theology is their starting points. Open theism has its origins within evangelicalism, and so seeks to root its position in Scripture, whereas process theology makes explicit use of the philosophical categories provided by Whitehead and Hartshorne to make contemporary sense of Scripture, tradition, and other sources that can help interpret the divine nature, presence, and purposes. Thus, there are many similarities in how the future is imagined, but the path to that vision is different. In the end, both are expressive of an open and relational vision of God and creation.

13

Continuing the Path toward Universal Restoration

Contemporary Eastern Orthodoxy and the Second Coming

The center of contemporary Orthodox eschatology is the resurrection of Jesus. This eschatological vision is most fully expressed in the Eucharist, which anticipates the kingdom banquet that the church expects to follow the second coming of Christ. As Andrew Louth puts it: "In gathering together, the early Christians looked forward to the coming of the kingdom; as they celebrated the Eucharist together, they knew themselves to be on the threshold of the kingdom."[1] This understanding of the relationship between the Eucharist and eschatology has deep roots in the theology of the Eastern Orthodox churches and finds expression in contemporary Orthodox theology.

The eschatological role of the Eucharist is rooted in the belief that the kingdom of God, as Alexander Schmemann writes, "is the content of the Christian faith—the goal, the meaning and the content of the Christian life.... The kingdom of God is unity with God, the source of all life, indeed life itself."[2] The Eucharist points to the coming of the kingdom and how it provides a taste of the kingdom in the present, as those gathered for worship commune in anticipation of sharing with Christ the heavenly banquet. So, as Schmemann writes, "each time that Christians 'assemble as the church' they witness before the whole world that Christ is King and Lord, that his kingdom has already been revealed and given to man and that a new and immortal life has begun."[3]

With the Eucharist serving as a reference point to Christ's coming kingdom, providing a foretaste of what is to come, as we have seen earlier, many Eastern Christians, following Origen, envisioned that at the coming of Christ the world would see the restoration of all things. There are differences in understanding what this entails. For some, this idea of *apokatastasis* (restoration of all things) is equated with some form of universal salvation. Others believe that the world will see the restoration of all things, but that does not mean all will be saved. As the Russian theologian Vladimir Lossky notes, "One can neither deny nor defend *apokatastasis*. The idea of it becomes heretical if one sees in it a certain divine determinism that denies the possibility of choice."[4]

Sergius Bulgakov, another important twentieth-century Russian Orthodox theologian, followed Origen more closely and spoke of the restoration of all things in terms of the beginning rather than the end, so that "nothing in the world is lost and nothing is annihilated except evil, conquered by the power of God and thereby exposed in its non-being. But the history of the world, which is the history of the church, is the building up of the realm of God, the City of God. And this can be called apocatastasis only in the sense of the universal salvation whose foundation was already laid when all that exists was created."[5]

As we think in terms of eschatology and the final restoration of all things, there is disagreement as to whether all will experience salvation. Nevertheless, there is continuity in the belief that our ultimate destiny is union with God, which, as we have seen, is understood in terms of deification or *theosis*.

We see the idea of *theosis* or deification in Athanasius's declaration that God became human so that humans might be God (that is, experience deification or immortality). We have seen how this idea was developed by Maximus the Confessor and Gregory Palamas. Their legacy is seen in modern Orthodox eschatology.

Concerning *theosis*, Vladimir Lossky builds on Palamas's concept of the distinction between the divine essence and the divine energies. The divine essence is transcendent and unknowable, but God is knowable through the divine uncreated energies. According to his interpretation of human nature, humans can be "partakers of the divine nature" (2 Pet. 1:4 KJV). That is, according to Lossky, the promise of union with God, which is our ultimate end. Regarding the divine energies, Lossky writes that "they are the outpourings of the divine nature which cannot set bounds to itself, for God is more than essence. The energies might be described as that mode of existence of the Trinity which is outside of its inaccessible essence."[6]

There is much more to this view of God that undergirds the vision of *theosis,* but this must suffice. Regarding humanity's ultimate end, the idea of *theosis* speaks of ultimate union with God. By that Lossky and others mean union with the energies of God, not with God's essence, which remains inaccessible to us. According to Lossky, *theosis* is fully realized in the age to come after the second coming of Christ, when all humanity, the living and the dead, face the day of judgment. While Orthodoxy envisions a final judgment, the process of deification (*theosis*) can begin in the present, "through the transformation of our corruptible and depraved nature and by its adaptation to eternal life." This occurs through our cooperation with God. The way to union involves "prayer, fasting, vigils, and other Christian practices," but not these only.

Regarding the Christian life and the way it is lived in relationship to the movement toward union with God, he writes, "The virtues are not the end but the means, or, rather, the symptoms, the outward manifestations of the Christian life, the sole end of which is the acquisition of grace."[7] There is also a sacramental dimension to this process. Lossky suggests, "We are deified each time we commune, but our eyes are not able to discern the glory that radiates from now on. The spiritual life is precisely the opening of our eyes to glory."[8] The issue here is not merit, which is not a major concern in the Eastern church. Rather, the focus is on synergy and cooperation with God. As a result, "grace is not a reward for the merit of the human will, as Pelagianism would have it; but no more is it the 'meritorious acts' of our free will. For it is not a question of merits but of cooperation, a synergy of the two wills, divine and human, a harmony in which grace bears ever more and more fruit, and is appropriated—'acquired'—by the human person."[9]

The path taken by Eastern churches looks very different from that of the churches in the West. The Eastern path tends to be less apocalyptic, though it has its apocalyptic dimensions. It envisions some form of restoration of all things though whether all humans will participate in this restoration is a matter of debate within the tradition. David Bentley Hart writes of the enduring affirmation, especially in the East, of universal salvation: "Belief in universal salvation may have been far more widespread in the first four or five centuries of Christian history than it was in all the centuries that followed; but it was never, as a rule, encouraged in any general way by those in authority in the church."[10] For most theologians in the Eastern churches, the eschatological hope is ultimately union with God, which involves deification (*theosis*), such that humanity joins with Divinity in eternal bliss.

As we have seen, the process by which the faithful move toward experiencing the fullness of God's Realm, which includes union with God, is expressed in prayer, contemplation, and worship, especially in partaking of the Eucharist, as it anticipates sharing the table with Christ in the kingdom. However the kingdom of God is understood, the ultimate goal is union with God in Christ, by which the faithful put on immortality (*theosis*).

SECTION FIVE

"Will the Real Afterlife Please Stand Up?"

Voices on the Life after Death

We've been talking about last things, including Jesus' second coming, but something very personal is included in the larger conversation. That something concerns the afterlife. What happens to us when we die? Is there something more to reality than this life? If so, what does it look like? In the following chapters, we're going to briefly explore some of the possible options. Some of them overlap, but others are quite distinct. Some of these perspectives have biblical roots, but ultimately each one involves interpretation. Many of us believe that it's ultimately impossible to *know* what lies ahead. In other words, we simply do not have empirical proof about what happens in the afterlife. However, many live in the hope that there is something more than this life, which is both reasonable and energizes their current life experience. While many Christians ponder what the future holds, others assume that we cannot know what happens in the afterlife, and that it's best to simply trust in God's grace and love and focus on the present life.

For our purposes, we've placed boundaries between several of these approaches as if they're clear and precise. We know that in actual practice these categories are not as well-defined as we portray them. We try to identify the distinguishing characteristics of each perspective, knowing that there is a lot of mixing and matching, especially at the popular level. We've chosen not to deal with viewpoints that don't have much traction in Christian tradition, such as reincarnation, though it has grown in popularity among some Christians. We've also chosen not to address the question of near-death experiences, as this subject is more complicated than we can take up in this book. We try to focus on the most commonly held views on the afterlife.

14

The Afterlife in the Old Testament

Some Christians think the concept of an afterlife is completely absent from the Old Testament, and the New Testament gives the earliest evidence of a full-bodied life beyond the grave. In fact, the views found in the Old Testament are diverse. Therefore, we should speak not of *the* Old Testament perspective but of Old Testament *perspectives* on the afterlife. While most of these forms are modest compared to later Christian views, Daniel 12:13 offers the first fully developed picture of the resurrection of the dead in the Bible.

Some Old Testament writers refer to postdeath human existence as "shades" (e.g., Ps. 88:10; Isa. 14:9; 26:14). These shades dwell in Sheol. It's not entirely clear how the shade was constituted, but the word "shade" suggests something shadowy. Some passages suggest a static existence. The ancients may have originally used Sheol to refer to little more than a common family grave. Many biblical writers envisioned Sheol as a bland, gray abode for the dead. It was an underworld lacking vibrancy of fully animated life in the world above. We see these themes in Psalm 88:10–12, which portrays the shades as being far removed from the presence of God. The psalmist, in a state of despondency, asks God:

> Do you work wonders for the dead?
>> Do the shades rise up to praise you?   *Selah*
> Is your steadfast love declared in the grave,
>> or your faithfulness in Abaddon?
> Are your wonders known in the darkness,
>> or your saving help in the land of forgetfulness?

For this psalmist, not only is Sheol bland and gray, but it's devoid of God's active presence (see also Ps. 6:5; Eccl. 9:10; Isa. 38:18). However, other voices describe Sheol as a place of activity and vitality. Thus, God can bring a person up from Sheol (Pss. 30:3; 49:15; 86:13) or even visit Sheol, with the shades rising to greet the creator (Isa. 14:9–15). God even could be present in Sheol, as the psalmist declared to God: "If I ascend to heaven, you are there; if I make my bed in Sheol, you are there" (Ps. 139:8).

Some passages suggest that God consigns people to Sheol because of their wickedness (e.g., Num. 16:33; 1 Kgs. 2:6–9; Pss. 9:17; 31:17; 55:15; 141:7). However, Old Testament writers typically stop short of portraying Sheol as a place of active, immediate, ongoing fiery punishment, which Christians later associate with hell.

There are a few references in the Old Testament that speak of contact between people living in this world and people who are dead. For example, although Saul cast mediums out of Israel (1 Sam. 28:3), fearing the Philistine army, Saul later sent a messenger to a medium asking that she bring back the prophet Samuel from the dead for a consultation. When Samuel appears, he rebukes Saul and predicts not only that Israel will be defeated, but that Saul and his sons will be killed (1 Sam. 28:4–19). Such activities are considered to be idolatry by many Old Testament writers (Deut. 18:10–11; Lev. 20:6; Isa. 8:19–22).

People looking for evidence of life after death in the Old Testament often point to Ezekiel's vision of the valley of dry bones as being an anticipation of the resurrection of the dead, though in its original context this passage refers to God regenerating the nation of Israel (Ezek. 37:1–14). The same can be said of Isaiah 26:19, where we read, "Your dead shall live, their corpses shall rise." Like Psalm 115:16–18 and Isaiah 38:18–19, these passages do point to the idea of the resurrection that becomes fully present in Daniel 12:1–3.

The apocalyptic story of Daniel—written around 168–165 BCE—speaks of the faithful suffering because of their witness in the face of opposition. The notion of resurrection emerges as the author tries to explain how God can keep God's promises to the faithful when they have endured great pain on God's behalf:

> At that time Michael, the great prince, the protector of your people, shall arise. There shall be a time of anguish, such as has never occurred since nations first came into existence. But at that time your people shall be delivered, everyone who is found written in the book. Many of those who sleep in the dust of the earth shall awake, some to everlasting life, and some to shame and everlasting contempt. Those who are wise shall shine like the brightness of the sky, and those who lead many to righteousness, like the stars forever and ever. (Dan. 12:1–3)

Daniel anticipates a series of events taking place in the not too distant future, when God will bring the dead back to life. At that time God will judge the living and the dead, sending some to punishment and others to a new life, thereby making things right for the faithful.

As we noted in chapter 1, Daniel was not the first to articulate such a point of view. Jewish authors put such thoughts into expression in documents written in the same general era as Daniel. These books include *1 Enoch*, *4 Ezra* (also known as *2 Esdras)*, and *Testament of the Twelve Patriarchs*. Moreover, again recalling chapter 1, we noticed that 2 Maccabees posits that the living faithful can pray on behalf of some of the unfaithful dead that God would raise the dead to eternal life on the last day (2 Macc. 12:41–45). Some later interpreters regarded this passage as the first mention of purgatory, though 2 Maccabees itself does not reveal that level of detail.

We comment more fully on the nature of the transition from present suffering to resurrection body in the next section. For now, it is enough to say that from the viewpoint of Daniel's vision of resurrection, the New Testament does not so much innovate as develop the idea further and connect it to Jesus.

15

The Resurrection of the Dead in the New Heaven and New Earth

In this chapter, we'll expand on what we've already discussed in chapters 2 and 14 regarding the resurrection of the body. We'll focus on the circumstances that gave rise to the idea of the resurrection of the body, as well as the historical development of this idea, which reminds us that the idea of resurrection didn't just drop out of thin air. Along the way, we'll lift up references to the resurrection present both in early Judaism and in the New Testament. The concept of resurrection from the dead is rooted in the Hebrew belief that a person is a unified whole and not a collection of parts (body, soul, and mind). Everything that makes up a person is interconnected. Therefore, a person does not *have* a body but *is* a body.

The resurrection of the dead is not an end in itself. It's part of a much larger apocalyptic hope that at the time of the second coming, God will bring into existence a new heaven and new earth (2 Pet. 3:1–10; Rev. 21:1–22:5). That is, God will re-create what exists so that God's purposes of love, justice, peace, and abundance can shape persons, relationships, and situations.

Resurrection in Early Judaism

As we observed in connection with Daniel 12 in the previous chapter, the idea of the resurrection of the dead emerged within the Jewish community as it wrestled with God's justice. They faced a dilemma because they believed God promised to bless those who lived according to the covenant. However, during times of conflict, many faithful Jews suffered and even died as martyrs. Some Jewish thinkers came to believe that if God was going to keep this promise, then God would need to create not only a new world but also new (resurrection) bodies for those who persevered in their witness despite experiencing suffering and even death because of their commitment to the cause.

While Daniel 12:1–3 is the only Old Testament passage to speak of the resurrection of the body, Jewish writers began moving in this direction as early as 300 BCE. Then late in the first century CE, shortly after the Romans destroyed the temple in Jerusalem in 70 CE, a book known as *2 Baruch* offers a representative description of the resurrection many people would have embraced. The sovereign God says:

> And it will happen after [God] has brought down everything that is in the world, and has sat down in eternal peace on the throne of the kingdom, then joy will be revealed and rest will appear. And then health will descend in dew, and illness will vanish, and fear and tribulation and lamentation will pass away from among [human beings], and joy will encompass the earth. And nobody will again die untimely, nor will any adversity take place suddenly . . . and the wild beasts will come from the wood and serve [human beings], . . . And women will no longer have pain when they bear, nor will they be tormented when they yield the fruits of their womb. (*2 Baruch* 73:1–3a, 6–7a)

In this scenario, when human beings die, they either lose consciousness altogether or go as a shade to Sheol to await the day of judgment. On that day God will bring the dead back to life and judge them along with the living, assigning those who remained steadfast during life, especially during difficult times, to "delight and rest . . . [and] only the splendor of the glory of the Most High," while those who are disobedient will be consigned to punishment. Thus, God does what is right by those who are true to the values and practices of the Realm of God.

Resurrection in the New Testament

Many followers of Jesus believed the day of judgment and resurrection would take place when Jesus returned in glory. This judgment would not be based simply on what one believed about Jesus but on how one lived in relation to the values of God's Realm.

Paul gives the fullest description of the resurrection body in 1 Corinthians 15. Beginning with the analogy of seed sprouting and growing, the apostle says, "God gives it a body as [God] has chosen, and to each kind of seed its own body" (1 Cor. 15:38). "There is one glory of the sun, and another glory of the moon, and another glory of the stars; indeed, star differs from star in glory" (1 Cor. 15:41). "So it is," Paul says, "with the resurrection of the dead" (1 Cor. 15:42a). The apostle then strains language to point to differences in quality between the present body and the resurrection body. "What is sown is perishable, what is raised is imperishable. It is sown in dishonor, it is raised in glory. It is sown in weakness, it is raised in power. It is sown a physical body, it is raised a spiritual body. If there is a physical body, there is also a spiritual body" (1 Cor. 15:42b–44). In this view, the "spiritual body" is a material body animated by the Spirit. Therefore, it is no longer subject to the vagaries of the old creation, including the threat of death.

The New Testament authors don't go into great detail when it comes to the specifics of life after death. Christians sometimes turn to the book of Revelation, especially the description of the New Jerusalem in Revelation 21:9–22:5, as a straightforward description of heaven. For example, it has streets of gold and high walls. But the author of Revelation uses the language of the city figuratively to point to qualities of the new heaven and the new earth and doesn't intend to give a blueprint of the life to come. John summarizes these qualities in more straightforward language in Revelation 21:1–8. For example, God will dwell with mortals, wiping away every tear, while ending pain and sorrow and death.

The New Testament addresses the contrast between the conditions that exist in this age and the future age. For example, in the Gospels, Jesus debates the Sadducees (who did not believe in the resurrection of the dead) over the fate of a woman whose husband died. According to the laws of levirate marriage, since this man had six brothers, she would become the wife of the next brother. If he died, she would become the wife of the next brother until her late husband had no more brothers to marry. The Sadducees ask Jesus, whose wife would she be in the resurrection? Jesus replies by saying: "For when they rise from the dead, they neither marry nor are given in marriage, but are like angels in heaven" (Mark 12:25; cf. Matt. 22:30; Luke 20:35). In the coming world, the inhabitants have bodies and live in conditions of "delight and rest . . . [and] the splendor of the glory of the Most High." The idea of the resurrection of the body does imply the regeneration of personal existence and awareness but, as is so clear in 1 Corinthians 15:35–58, the nature of existence itself is transformed.

In the background is the idea that what happens in and through the body is of ultimate importance both in this life and the next. Therefore, the way people embody the theology and ethics of the Realm of God in the old world shapes what happens in and through their bodies in the world to come.

16

The Soul Goes to Heaven

Although New Testament writers most commonly speak of the resurrection of the body, the belief that the soul goes to heaven after death was widespread in Greek circles in the centuries before and after Jesus. Some Jewish groups adapted this idea, often mixing the ideas of an immortal soul and the resurrection of the body. Echoes of the immortality of the soul appear, at least in the background, in the Gospel and Letters of John, as well as in Hebrews.

This idea that the soul goes to heaven at death is probably the most common way people envision the afterlife. The Greek philosopher Plato offered an influential expression of the idea that the soul and body are two separable parts. Humans are composed of a material/physical body and a nonmaterial soul. The soul resembles electricity, which is essentially invisible to the human eye, but it powers such things as lightbulbs and motors. Similarly, the soul not only animates the body but contains the essence of the person. This includes the mind. Thus, when death comes, the soul separates from the body and goes to heaven, while the body disintegrates. In this model, heaven is a place separate from the earth, where God and other heavenly beings (such as angels and souls) dwell. The soul, which includes the person's earthly identity, lives on in the presence of God, along with the angels and other souls.

This view is different from the gnostic viewpoint, which sometimes seeps into contemporary discussions of the afterlife. The gnostics were active in the second century CE (probably after most of the New Testament had been written). They believed not only that the body would separate from the soul, but also that the body—like the rest of the physical world—is evil. Because the soul is trapped in the body, it needs to be liberated from its imprisonment in the body. This liberation occurs at death. While this negative view of the body seeped into some Christian teaching in the second century and afterward, it's not characteristic of either the Old or New Testament.

Many Christians expect that when they go to heaven, they'll be reunited with family and friends so they can continue these earthly relationships in heaven. Serious Christian interpreters are divided on this issue, but the New Testament doesn't explicitly speak of this possibility. Supporters of this position believe it's *implied* in biblical passages, most of which assume the resurrection of the body. This expectation is most commonly found in the Gospel and Letters of John.

As we noted in chapter 2, the Gospel of John divides existence into two spheres: heaven above and the earth below. God dwells in heaven. Heaven is marked by love, life, light, peace, truth, freedom, and grace. By contrast, Satan lives in the world below, which is marked by hate, death, darkness, violence, lying, slavery, and legalism.

While the barrier between heaven and earth is pretty firm, God loves the world below and sent Jesus to be the means of salvation for those who believe (e.g., John 3:13–16). John speaks in terms of the Word of God (Logos) becoming flesh and dwelling in this world (John 1:14). After dwelling in the world for a time, Jesus ascends (returns) to heaven (e.g., John 3:13; 6:62; 20:17). At his resurrection, Jesus' identity changed so that he could ascend. Mary didn't recognize Jesus when she first saw him after the resurrection, mistaking him for the gardener (John 20:15).

Whatever the nature of the substance of the resurrected Jesus, it was pliable enough that he could slip through a wall to be with the disciples in their upper room (John 20:19, 26), and yet, at the same time, Thomas could touch Jesus (John 20:26–30).

John indicates that the disciples will follow Jesus to heaven, ascending just as he ascended (John 14:1–7). Jesus will return for the disciples (John 14:3–4). While the Johannine Jesus doesn't give a detailed description of heaven, he does speak of there being "many dwelling places" in God's house. This is welcome news in a world where travelers often were at significant risk, especially if they couldn't find lodging for the night. Fortunately, a place of safety awaits in heaven.

The Johannine community didn't need to wait for the last day to begin experiencing the qualities of eternal life. Those who believed in Jesus could begin enjoying the qualities of eternal life in this life (e.g., John 3:15–16, 36; 4:14; 5:24; 6:40, 47, 54; 10:28; 12:25; 17:3). Indeed, those who believe in Jesus will not die but will transition from life in this world to live in heaven with Jesus. This view is present in John 11, where Jesus' friend Lazarus has died and has lain in the tomb four days before Jesus arrives. When Jesus tells Lazarus's sister Martha, "Your brother will rise again," she replies, "I know that he will rise again in the resurrection on the last day" (John 11:23–24).

While Martha voices the conventional thinking of those who believe in the resurrection of the dead, Jesus tells her, "I am the resurrection and the life. Those who believe in me, even though they die, will live, and everyone who lives and believes in me will never die" (John 11:25–26). In the Gospel of John, Jesus not only reinforces the view that believing in him brings the qualities of eternal life into operation now, but Jesus also indicates that those who believe in him will never die; they will continue to live. This perspective contrasts with the notion of the resurrection of the dead, which assumes that at death consciousness ceases and the body, the individual, lies inert, awaiting the resurrection.

17

Soul and Body Separated at Death but Reunited and Transformed in Heaven

For some, the resurrection of the body and the soul going to heaven are combined. In this view, Jesus' second coming plays a key role. In this framework, the body and the soul are separate entities. While both are essential if we wish to flourish in this life, at death the soul leaves the body. It may go immediately to heaven or to an intermediate state where the soul is purified. In the Roman Catholic tradition, this is known as purgatory. Orthodoxy envisions an intermediate state, but it simply serves as a place of waiting until the day of judgment, when a person is assigned either to heaven or to hell.

As for the body, it waits in the ground or disintegrates. Thus, each person might be conscious either in heaven or the intermediate state, but until they are reunited with their body, they remain incomplete. When Jesus returns to the world, God raises the body from the earth, transforms it into a resurrection body, and reunites it with the soul. The resurrected/reunited individual then stands before God's judgment before being consigned to an eternal future in the Realm of God or in hell.

A common question concerns the fate of the body. If it decomposes—or is cremated—so that little or nothing is left of it, then what will be resurrected? One answer is that if God can create a world, then God can re-create a body for life in a new heaven and new earth. Augustine responded to this question in his *Enchiridion,* suggesting that at the moment of the resurrection, each person will be restored to their normal human form, "so that each soul will have its own body." As for what happens if a body has turned to ash or vapors, he wrote that "the earthly material from which mortal flesh is created" does not "perish from the sight of God." Indeed, "whatever dust or ashes it may dissolve into, whatever vapors or winds it may vanish into, whatever other bodies or even elements it may be turned into, by whatever animals or even men it may have been eaten as food and so turned into flesh, in an instant of time it returns to the human soul that first gave it life so that it might become human, grow, and live."[1]

18

The Spiritual Journey
toward Union with God

Eastern Orthodox Christianity differs from Western churches at points in its understanding of humanity's ultimate destiny. While there are continuities between Eastern and Western thinking, and between past and present, the Eastern churches have their own distinct beliefs. Careful readers also will see similarities between the Gospel of John and the Orthodox tradition. This is because both John and the Orthodox churches are influenced in different degrees and ways by certain Greek patterns of thinking.

Orthodoxy tends to approach the last things, including the resurrection, liturgically. Thus, the Eucharist is celebrated in anticipation of sharing the messianic banquet in the Realm of God. One should pray looking east, in expectation of Christ's return. Andrew Louth writes: "The Orthodox Church lives in the hope of the coming again of Christ in glory, as the creed affirms, and of all that is bound up with this second coming: the Final Judgement, the resurrection of the dead, the transfiguration of the cosmos. All this is determined by the life on the threshold of the kingdom, experienced in the eucharistic celebration."[1]

As noted above, at least on a popular level, the expectation is that at death one enters an intermediate state where one awaits the coming of Christ and the final judgment, at which point a person is assigned either heaven or hell.

When it comes to the believer's ultimate destiny, many Orthodox Christians use the word *theosis* to describe a person's spiritual journey toward union with God. The Greek word *theosis* can be translated as "divinization" or "deification." *Theosis* can be best understood in terms of our movement through life toward union with God. Norman Russell defines *theosis* as "our restoration as persons to integrity and wholeness by participation in Christ through the Holy Spirit, in a process which is initiated in this world through our life of ecclesial communion and moral striving and finds ultimate fulfillment in our union with the Father—all within the broad context of the divine economy."[2]

When it comes to union with God, Orthodox Christianity distinguishes between union with God's essence, which is unknowable, and union with God's uncreated energies. Union with God is understood to be a lifelong process, often accomplished through asceticism and contemplation, but it can be undertaken in more activist ways as well. In some ways, this is similar to the process of sanctification, but it is more than simply sanctification.

The process of *theosis* is a journey involving three phases. The first phase involves purification. Believers seek to purge the mind of the things that tempt. Believers seek to get their passions or appetites under control so that they do not distract the believer. The second phase is illumination. Believers seek to become better able to recognize and respond to the things of God. Believers seek to grow in understanding of God, in love, and in the fullness of the divine qualities. The third phase is the way of union. The believer is now significantly in union with God in the way described above. Believers are restored to the quality of relationship with God and life. Christians who are in union with God in this life are experiencing something similar to the state about which the Johannine Jesus referred when saying that those who believe in Jesus have eternal life already.

For Orthodox churches, *theosis* is an unending process, even after death. A human being—a created entity—can never arrive, in the sense of being completely like the uncreated God. As for the resurrection, Orthodoxy teaches that at death, the soul and the body are separated. At death, the soul moves to an intermediate state, while the body decays. When Christ returns, the soul will be reunited with the body. When this occurs, the person (united soul and body) is transformed into an imperishable physical reality in the same way that the risen Christ has an imperishable physical reality. The general resurrection is followed by the final judgment, where the faithful experience God's love fully and uninterruptedly while others experience condemnation.

While Orthodoxy contains the idea of hell, there is also a strong universalist stream, going back to Origen, that looks to the restoration of all things (*apokatastasis pantōn*). As Andrew Louth notes, "The grounds for this are principally the long-suffering love of God for all creation, and also the conviction that evil is without substance, but is rather a corruption or distortion of what is good."[3] Thus, while there is still among some the expectation that hell could be in one's future, there is also the prospect that God will become all in all, and thus all will be restored.

19

Afterlife as Consciousness in the Consciousness of God

Adherents of process theology hold two views on the afterlife. One group thinks that after death the believer's consciousness remains conscious in God. The other group believes that at death, humans lose consciousness, but a person's life continues to affect the flow of experience in the world. We take up this viewpoint in the next chapter, "The End of Consciousness."

Process thinkers—like many others—believe the language and worldview of the Bible, and a good bit of Christian tradition, reflect ancient worldviews. In this ancient worldview, many believed in a three-storied universe—heaven above, earth in the middle, and an underworld below. The ancients further believed that human beings are composed of both the soul and the body. In that context, it makes sense to speak of a person's destination after death in terms of going to heaven above or hell below. Process thinkers accept the current scientific view that the universe is infinitely expanding. Therefore, it doesn't make sense to speak of defined spaces such as heaven. Of course, we can speak figuratively of "up" and "down," but where would heaven be located for a soul to experience the afterlife?

Process thinkers imagine God's relationship with the world as one in which all things take place in God. Therefore, God is not external to people, animals, and the elements of nature. While the analogy is imperfect, it moves toward a visual representation: God and the world are like a snow globe in which God is the globe and the glycerin (the water substance inside the snow globe), while the world is the contents of the snow globe (e.g., miniature children, a snow clown, trees, a rabbit).

However, in contrast to the snow globe, God and the world are in a dynamic relationship in which they affect one another. In real life, God is not an inflexible shell and impermeable glycerin. God is affected by what people do and by what happens in nature. In turn, God affects people and nature. In this conceptualization, God's capacity to be aware of others—God's memory—is infinite. So, when it comes to the afterlife, God remembers everything that happens in the world. Concerning people, God remembers every thought and every action. Because the memory of God is alive, God does not simply recall the past as chunks; God feels the things of the past.

The thoughts and feelings that make up a person do not die. They continue to live in God. Therefore, human consciousness doesn't disappear when the body ceases to function. Consciousness continues as a personal consciousness in the life of God. Those who have died physically can thus be aware of other entities whose consciousnesses are alive in God. The afterlife of the human being, then, is to be aware of one's own awareness, to be aware of one's life in God, and to be aware of other consciousnesses in God. The person's consciousness lives forever, but it doesn't dwell in a specific place other than in God's consciousness. But in this way of thinking, who we are and what we have done goes on because it is alive in God.

20

The End of Consciousness

Some people think that at death people simply lose consciousness forever. The brain ceases functioning. The heart stops. The body decomposes. There is no soul to continue conscious living. Eventually, there is nothing left of the person. It is as if a person is a lamp, and someone turns off the switch. Survivors are left with their memories but no expectation of interacting with the deceased again.

We sometimes associate this view with atheists. But some Christians affirm this perspective, including a group of process thinkers who introduce an important nuance. According to the process conception of God, God receives everything that happens in history and carries it forward. In the process view, life is not a static entity but is an endless series of events that are constantly evolving. Life is a series of moments in which things come together from the past to create a meaningful occasion The moment occurs, and then what occurred at the moment becomes a resource for the next moment. Resources from the past—everything that has gone before—come into the present, where inhabitants intentionally or unintentionally create the moment. What they create flows forward as something the creators of the next moment might, intentionally or unintentionally, use in forming the next moment. The moment brings certain possibilities to expression while leaving other possibilities unexpressed. These movements can happen very fast. Indeed, as this sentence is being typed, the moment with which the typing began is already evolving into the next moment.

As we noted in the previous section, God carries the past forward as part of the flow of history. Everything we think or do is included in the past and is available as a resource for the present. Although people may die, the way they have affected the world doesn't disappear. In this sense, they live on. Later generations may not be explicitly aware of specific people and their particular contributions to life. Even when later generations don't know about particular contributions on the part of particular people to the great flow of life, those contributions are still in the great, deep flux of life and therefore are available to help shape ongoing experience. The good I do offers the possibility of good for the future. Of course, the opposite is true. The evil that I do now continues to offer the possibility of evil for individuals and communities in the future.

On the one hand, thinking about the afterlife in terms of the resources one leaves in the flow of life may not be as immediately inviting as being raised from the dead into a restored world or as the soul journeying to heaven to dwell with other souls. On the other hand, this way of thinking gives lasting meaning to everything we do. As one of our colleagues said, "Everything we do matters because it leaves an effect. Somebody will pick up on that effect someday, even if they don't know they are picking it up." Someone else said, "What we do is ultimately important because they matter to the one who is ultimate." When considering human communities, nature, and the world itself, this notion of the afterlife prompts us to ask, "What kind of world do we want to leave for people and plants and everything else?"

Concluding Thoughts

The future can be anxiety-producing, even for Christians. We may embrace the message of 1 John that perfect love casts out fear (1 John 4:18), and yet we often carry with us a fear of the unknown. In this book, we have attempted to share some insights when it comes to ways in which Christians past and present have envisioned the future. As we've shown in the course of the book, there is more than one way of looking at these questions. We've tried to provide information drawn from Scripture, history (tradition), and current perspectives, that can assist in developing one's eschatology. We have our own beliefs on these matters (and we don't agree on everything).

Since you made it this far, we invite you to identify what you believe about the second coming, God's ultimate purposes, and the afterlife. You'll want to think about whether your understanding of these issues has changed as you've read and reflected on what you found in the book. We would encourage you to ask the question as to what difference your view of such things makes in the way you view God and the world. What are the real-world implications?

In our process of discernment regarding these matters, it's important to take into consideration the way we interpret the Bible, the way we respond to the voices of Christian tradition, and our own experience of the world. Each of us brings different experiences to these questions, which can make the process of discernment a bit messy.

From our perspective, as authors of this book, we believe that the way we understand God will influence the choices we make. We also believe that as Christians, Jesus sets the standard for determining our beliefs about the future. We believe that the biblical declaration that God is love should guide our work of discernment. If our belief systems don't lead toward justice and mercy, then are they expressions of *Christian* eschatology?

We have tried to address a very complicated set of questions concerning differences of opinion and perspective. We believe that showing respect for others doesn't mean we always agree with one another. There is a place for strong debate on these questions, because they are important questions. There is a joke that goes around when it comes to these questions and issues. It has to do with panmillennialism. In other words, it'll pan out in the end. That is true, but that doesn't mean we shouldn't take these questions seriously. While we can't predict the future, we all contribute to the way the future unfolds.

One of the reasons why we decided to take up this topic is that we saw it being neglected in mainline Protestant churches, like the ones we are part of. And we also saw how certain perspectives have contributed to conspiracy theories, degradation of the environment, neglect of social justice, and embracing authoritarian modes of government. Having a good handle on the various perspectives can help us discern the interpretations that are most plausible so that we can avoid embracing perspectives that demean and destroy. Once again, as the authors of this study, we believe strongly that God is present and active in the world seeking to bring about love, peace, justice, dignity, freedom, and abundance, and that God is in partnership with God's people.

We must remember that we as human beings are finite. Our capacity for understanding has its limits. Even when we know something, we do not always know *everything* there is to know about it. In the strict sense, the human family cannot be positively certain about what will happen in the future when it comes to the second coming, God's ultimate purposes for humankind and nature, or the afterlife. What we can do is commit ourselves to making good use of contemporary biblical scholarship and theology as we pursue these questions. As we do this, we can follow the admonition of Micah, who answers the question as to what God requires of us: "to do justice, and to love kindness, and to walk humbly with your God" (Mic. 6:8).

Study Guide

Introduction

We, the authors, believe that this book is valuable for both individual reading and small group discussions. Before beginning the study series, we recommend that leaders and readers look through the glossary, so they are familiar with key terms such as "eschatology" and "apocalypse." Having this background information will make the conversation flow more easily and be more meaningful.

Each participant in the group should have a copy of the book so they can prepare for the conversation. While not every session focuses on the Bible, having a copy of the Bible for each session is also important. We encourage group leaders to adapt the questions in the guide to their context. It's not necessary to cover every question.

We believe that prayer is constitutive of the Christian life. Because this conversation sometimes touches on sensitive matters, we think it is especially important that it be carried out in the context of prayer. We encourage the group to begin and end the sessions with prayer.

While this guide is organized around six sessions, groups may decide to extend the conversation over a larger period. The book itself is divided into five sections. Section Two of the book, the historical section, is divided into two sessions. You may want to divide session 1, dealing with the biblical section, into two sessions.

Each session in this six-week series invites readers to think about how they envision the future and whether Jesus will return at some point. If so, what might that look like? We also invite the readers to consider questions about the afterlife.

- Session 1 focuses on some introductory questions and the biblical materials.
- Session 2 picks up the conversation about God's ultimate purposes in the second century CE and then moves forward along an Eastern trajectory from the third-century theologian Origen to the fall of Constantinople (Istanbul) to the Ottomans and the rise of Russian Orthodoxy.
- Session 3 takes a similar journey, only this time it's the Western churches that we explore. We begin once again in the third century CE and journey toward the nineteenth century.
- Session 4 takes up the three primary millennialist traditions (Section Three): premillennialism, postmillennialism, and amillennialism. Here we will offer questions that will enable users to consider which, if any, of these theories help make sense of their own understandings of how the Realm of God might come into existence. This section is important because much of the conversation in our day on such matters is rooted in millennial theories.
- Session 5 invites readers/users to consider different ways in which some people today understand and envision the Realm of God.
- Session 6 invites readers to ponder ways in which Christians have understood questions about the afterlife.

As a general rule, we think people remain engaged in sessions that last about an hour or an hour and a half. But, of course, levels of interest vary from group to group.

Session 1: Voices from the Bible

This session focuses on Section One, "'I Wish We'd All Been Ready': Voices from the Bible." In the book, this material is found on pages 9–33.

1. The technical term for what we'll be studying in this book is "eschatology." As we point out in the book, the word "eschatology" means "study of the last things" or "study of God's final aims for human beings and the world." Eschatology is a category of theology that covers different aspects of the future, including the second coming of Jesus, the kingdom/Realm of God, the afterlife, and the final judgment.

- What comes to mind when you think about the possibility of a second coming? The possibility of a final judgment? What do you think happens after death?
- What feelings does thinking about the future in these ways evoke for you?
- On a spectrum about the future ranging from anxious to hopeful, where do you see yourself?
- What questions do you bring to this study?

2. In the introduction the authors speak of three things to keep in mind as you read through the book. What are these three things, and how might they help you think about the future as a Christian?

3. What does the Old Testament (see pp. 11-19) say about God's ultimate purposes for humanity and all of God's creation?

4. How do the Torah (first five books of the Old Testament), the Prophets, and the Writings speak of God's ultimate purposes?

- What similarities and differences do you notice in the different points of view?
- How might this diversity of perspective influence your understanding of the future?

5. The authors note that the Jewish community did not begin to contemplate the end times until the time of the exile.

- What is the message of these texts, especially the book of Daniel?
- How should we read these texts? Do they have implications for the far distant future?

– Might they speak to our own experience of the future reign of God?

6. Most Protestants do not include 1 and 2 Maccabees among the canonical books of the Old Testament. (The Anglican and Episcopal churches are exceptions in that they do recognize canonicity of these books). In any event, 1 and 2 Maccabees depict Jews who experienced a time of oppression and suffering in the years 168 to 165 BCE. In these books questions about the resurrection of the dead emerge. What do we learn about the resurrection, and how have these books influenced later developments in the Christian community?

Note: *Beginning with question 7, we move to the New Testament (pp. 20–33). If you choose to divide this section into two sessions, please begin the new session with a word of prayer. Then review the previous week's conversation before moving into the New Testament questions.*

7. The New Testament writers incorporate Jewish apocalyptic thinking into their vision of Jesus and the Realm of God (pp. 20–33).

– How is this Realm understood and portrayed in the New Testament?
– How do early Christians differentiate their views from their Jewish origins?
– What might the New Testament vision of God's Realm mean for us?

8. Paul's letters are the earliest written expressions of Christianity. There are strong apocalyptic elements to his theology.

– How does he understand the Realm of God, the second coming, and God's purposes?
– Is Paul's message authoritative for us? If so, what does this mean for us?

9. Written a generation after Paul, the Synoptic Gospels (Matthew, Mark, and Luke) provide a look at Jesus' view of the Realm of God.

- What is the message of these Gospels concerning Jesus' vision of God's purposes?
- How are they similar and different?
- With this in mind, how do you understand Jesus' vision as applied to us?

10. Continuing with the previous conversation, how do the Gospels incorporate apocalyptic elements into the story of Jesus, and how do you interpret this usage?

11. The book of Revelation, like Daniel 7–12, is an apocalypse.

- How does John, the author, envision the second coming?
- Placing the book in its historical context of the first century CE, what might we take from its apocalyptic imagery?

12. Jude and 2 Peter are lesser-known New Testament texts, but they also speak to God's ultimate purposes. What are your takeaways from these short letters?

13. The Johannine literature (Gospel and Letters) offers a rather distinct vision of the future, one that is less apocalyptic.

- How would you describe the Johannine view?
- How does this differ from Paul or the Synoptics?
- What feelings does the Johannine view evoke?
- What might we take from this literature?

Session 2: Voices in Christian Tradition: Eastern Trajectory (100–1600)

This session focuses on the first part of Section Two, "A Path toward Universal Restoration: The Eastern Christian Church." In the book this material is found on pages 35–56.

1. As early Christianity moved into the second century, it was spreading widely and including increasing numbers of Gentile converts. Many of the earlier New Testament apocalyptic visions continued, but they were often modified as time passed. We will follow two trajectories, one Eastern and one Western. However, in the earliest decades, running through the end of the second century, much was held in common. Two important contributors to the conversation are Justin Martyr and Irenaeus.

- What was the message proclaimed or revealed in the works of second-century theologians such as Justin and Irenaeus?
- How were their views similar to—and different from—those expressed in the New Testament?

2. Living at the beginning of the third century, Origen of Alexandria was a creative and influential theologian, setting the narrative for future generations when it comes to matters of the future.

- What are Origen's primary concerns when it comes to God's ultimate purposes?
- Discuss his response to earlier apocalyptic messages, including his understanding of the second coming.
- How does he set the agenda for future conversations?

3. Origen is known for his emphasis on the ultimate restoration of all things.

- What does he mean by restoration?
- How is this concept developed over time by later theologians, such as Gregory of Nyssa regarding universal salvation and Maximus the Confessor's emphasis on union with God (including the concept of *theosis*)?

4. As time passed, Christianity became a more prominent and eventually legal religious movement, which led to some embracing asceticism. How does asceticism express visions of God's Realm?

5. Although Origen and many of his followers de-emphasized apocalypticism, apocalypticism reemerged later in the early church period.

- How did Justinian and his successors use apocalyptic ideas to enhance imperial authority? Does this surprise you?
- What are some of the keys to these developments, including visions of the Realm of God (for example, the idea of the Last Roman Emperor)?
- Do people continue to do this kind of thing today? If so, where do you see it?

6. While the rise of Islam contributed to developing apocalyptic concerns in both Eastern and Western churches, Islam itself has apocalyptic dimensions.

- What does Islamic apocalypticism look like, and how does it relate to Christian expectations?
- While Jesus figures in Christian eschatology, how does he also figure in Islamic eschatology?

7. While Maximus the Confessor explored the idea of union with God as our ultimate destiny, several centuries later Gregory Palamas took this further. Discuss Gregory's vision of participating in the divine nature and how it relates to God's ultimate purposes.

8. In the mid-fifteenth century, the city of Constantinople (Istanbul) and with it the last remnants of the Byzantine (Eastern Roman) Empire fell to the Ottoman Empire (an Islamically oriented empire).

- How did this event give rise to apocalyptic concerns in the Christian world?

– What were some of the ramifications of this event for Eastern Orthodoxy?
– How did this event contribute to the growing influence of Russia on Eastern Orthodoxy?
– How is Russia's influence within Orthodoxy expressed in the modern world?

Session 3: Historical Voices— The Western Trajectory

This session focuses on two chapters in Section Two: chapter 4, "Settling In for the Long Haul: Views of the Second Coming in the Christian West," and chapter 5, "Still Here after All These Years: Views of the Second Coming in the Reformation and Beyond." In the book, this material is found on pages 57–74.

1. While Eastern Christianity, following Origen, tended to downplay apocalyptic imagery, Western Christianity, following Hippolytus, Tertullian, and Cyprian, continued the earlier thinking concerning the millennium and the second coming.

– What message did these early thinkers offer?
– Where do you see their influence today?

2. While there was a continuation of earlier millennial thought in the West, Augustine, writing in the fifth century, offered a different, more spiritualized trajectory that would prove influential over time. What was Augustine's position, and what influenced him in this direction?

3. While Augustine offered a spiritualized eschatology that would influence mainstream Catholic thinking, other, more apocalyptic movements emerged over the next thousand years. What were some of these movements and what led to their emergence?

4. Among the leading apocalyptic figures was the twelfth-century theologian Joachim of Fiore.

– What was Joachim's message?
– How did Joachim's message influence later developments?

5. We take Augustine and Joachim of Fiore as representative figures for understanding Western eschatological developments. When we come to the late fifteenth to the early sixteenth century:

– What events emerged that would lead to radical change in the West?
– Who are leading figures, and why did they emerge?

6. The origins of the Reformation come with the ministry of Martin Luther.

– What do we know about Luther's eschatology?
– Does Luther follow Augustine or Joachim more in his orientation?
– What do you make of his perspective on the second coming and God's ultimate purposes?

7. If Luther represents the origins of the Reformation, John Calvin is another influential early Reformed leader. What is Calvin's message when it comes to the second coming and God's ultimate purposes?

8. Luther and Calvin represent the "magisterial reformation," what we might call the mainstream perspective. However, they were not alone in their reforming efforts.

– When we turn to the Radical Reformation (including Anabaptism), what are some of the expressions of this movement when it comes to these questions?
– What are the positive notes and the negative ones of this broad movement?
– What can we learn from them about the way we understand God's involvement with the world and its future?

9. Many North American religious developments have their roots in English Puritanism. What was the Puritan perspective, and how did it express itself in England and North America?

Session 4: The Millennial Voices

The material for this session is found in Section Three, "'Are We Going to Be "Left Behind"?': The Millennial Voices," pages 75–93.

1. To this point we've looked at both the biblical and the historical materials that contribute to contemporary eschatological and apocalyptic thinking. Central to many conversations is the question of the millennium and how it should be interpreted. What is the key biblical text behind millennial thinking, and why is it important?

2. While not the most prominent millennial interpretive scheme today, postmillennialism has a strong pedigree that is rooted in earlier thinking (pp. 86–90).

– What is postmillennialism, and what are the most prominent expressions of this movement?
– As you ponder this question, where do you see this perspective present in our contemporary world religiously and politically?

3. If postmillennialism is one possible scheme, premillennialism is another. It has deep roots in history and Scripture. It is often seen as *the* biblical perspective (pp. 81–85).

– What are the major elements of modern premillennialism?
– The most prominent expression of this perspective is dispensationalism (pp. 78–80). What is dispensationalism? What are its key elements?
– Where do you find this perspective present in our contemporary world, and what might its influence be?

4. The third perspective is known as amillennialism (pp. 91–93). It too has deep historical roots.

– What are those roots?
– What is its basic message?

5. As you look at these three perspectives on the millennium, do any of them resonate with you? If so, why? If not, why not?

Session 5: Voices from the Contemporary World

This session covers five chapters, each of which focuses on a particular movement with eschatological implications. The questions will invite discussion of each movement, with the final question inviting participants to discuss which, if any, best fit their own understanding of God's ultimate purposes, and why. The material for this session is in Section Four in the book, "'How Do We Make Sense of the Second Coming Today?': Contemporary Voices," pages 95–121.

1. Chapter 9 focuses on demythologization, a movement linked to the twentieth-century theologian Rudolf Bultmann (pp. 97–101).

- What does Bultmann mean by demythologizing the Bible?
- In answering that question, what does he mean by myth?
- What are the implications for our discussion of the second coming, apocalypticism, the afterlife, and God's ultimate purposes?

2. Chapter 10 focuses on how God's future is realized in the present in the work of theologian Jürgen Moltmann and his theology of hope (pp. 102–5).

- How does Moltmann envision the future, and how does this influence the present? How does it offer hope?
- With his future orientation, how does Moltmann envision God's ultimate purposes? How will these purposes be experienced?

3. In chapter 11 we turn to liberation theology, which has some similarities to Moltmann's vision of God's purposes (pp. 106–11). What is liberation theology, and how does it understand God's ultimate purposes?

- What is the starting point for the various forms of liberation theology?
- What does God's Realm look like and encompass in this perspective?
- What role does Jesus play in this vision of God's Realm? Is this movement ultimately concerned about the second coming of Jesus?
- If liberation and the search for justice are central to God's ultimate purposes, how does the vision come to pass in the present age?

4. Chapter 12 explores two versions of open and relational theology when it comes to God's purposes (pp. 112–17).

- What are the two perspectives that fall under this category, and how do they understand the future?
- Discuss the similarities and differences between the two perspectives described here.
- How does the second coming factor into each perspective?
- If the future is open, how do they see this playing out over time?

5. Returning to our earlier exploration of the Eastern trajectory or tradition, we now focus on modern developments within Eastern Orthodoxy when it comes to eschatology (pp. 118–21).

- What does the future look like in Orthodoxy? What is central?
- How does the role of the Eucharist in Orthodox theology reflect Orthodox understandings of God's future?
- One aspect of Orthodox understandings of the future involves what is known as *theosis*. What is *theosis* and how does it reflect Orthodox understandings of God's future for humanity and the world?
- Diving deeper into this conversation about the restoration of all things and *theosis*, how might some Orthodox theologians understand salvation, more specifically, universal salvation?

6. Having explored and discussed each of the above contemporary perspectives, which one(s) match your own thinking? Which are intriguing? Which ones are problematic to you? Why?

Session 6: The Afterlife

The material for this session is found in Section Five of the book, "'Will the Real Afterlife Please Stand Up?': Voices on the Life after Death," pages 123–44.

1. Before discussing the different perspectives offered in Section Five related to the afterlife, discuss the perspective you brought to the group before reading the book.

– Did you come to this study believing there is an afterlife?
– Why? Why not?
– If yes, what did you think the afterlife would be like?

2. The authors touched on the way the Old Testament writers understood the afterlife, but in chapter 14, they focus on how these writers spoke of the afterlife (pp. 125–28).

– One concept present throughout the Old Testament is Sheol. What is Sheol? What does it look like? Does it offer hope? Or not?
– How does the book of Daniel offer a different perspective?
– In what ways do we see Daniel's vision in the New Testament?

3. In chapter 15 the authors turn to the question of the resurrection and the concept of a new heaven and a new earth (pp. 129–32).

– What are the sources of the developing Christian understanding of the resurrection?
– How is the resurrection understood in Judaism in the centuries just before the New Testament, and about the same time as the New Testament, including in the book of Daniel?

- How is the resurrection understood in the New Testament?
- How is the concept of the resurrection related to ideas about the second coming of Jesus?

4. As we turn to chapter 16, we see a different development, the idea of the soul going to heaven (pp. 133–35).

- What does it mean for the soul to go to heaven?
- If Sheol is prominent in the Old Testament and resurrection in early Judaism and the New Testament, where does the idea of resurrection come from? What are the sources and influences?
- How might this view relate to the concept of the resurrection?

5. In chapter 17, the authors discuss concepts of the soul being separated from the body at death and then at some point being reunited (pp. 129–37).

- In what ways does this concept relate to the previous discussions of resurrection and the soul?
- Why might this view be attractive to many Christians?

6. In chapter 18, we turn again to Eastern Orthodoxy and the concept of *theosis* (pp. 138–40).

- What are the three phases of *theosis*, and how does one experience deification? What does that mean?
- Why might this perspective be attractive not only to Orthodox persons but to people from across the Christian world, including Protestants?

7. In chapter 19, the authors review a position described as open theology (pp. 141–42; cf pp. 112–17).

- What are the core ideas in open theology with respect to the extent of God's power and the second coming?

- How do you feel about the idea that God could have absolute power and could intervene in the world, but God chooses not to do so until the second coming?

8. In chapter 19, the authors introduce perspectives connected to process theology (pp. 141–42).

- Some process thinkers conceive of the afterlife as the consciousness of the human being remaining alive in the consciousness of God. How do you respond to this possibility?
- Other thinkers, including some process thinkers, do not believe in an afterlife. Chapter 20 (pp. 143–44), discussing this view, suggests that when we die, all forms of our existence disappear. When we die, that is it. How do you respond to this possibility?

10. Do any of these differing perspectives speak to you as an individual?

- Do you find one or more of them attractive? If so, which ones, and why?
- Are you troubled by one or more of these views? If so, which ones, and why?
- What has happened to your thinking—if anything—as a result of engaging in this study? After encountering these views, are you reinforced in your thinking? Do you have different understandings? Do you have lingering questions?

A Final Word

We, the authors, hope that these sessions have opened new conversations and perhaps answered questions that have been on one's heart and mind. Our goal has been to inform, and while we have tried to be fair and honest, we hope we have persuaded you to dive more deeply into these questions for the good of the world we inhabit.

Glossary

Amillennialism: The belief that the millennium of Revelation 20:4–6 is a figurative expression and not a literal expectation. The millennium is generally understood in terms of Christ's reign through the church until the final judgment and the coming of the new heaven and the new earth. Many amillennialists believe that Christ will return; their expectation is open-ended as to when.

Antichrist: A figure who will arise in the last days to oppose Christ and lead a rebellion against God. The term is found only in 1 John 2:18, 22; 4:2–3; and 2 John 7, though some have seen other passages as associated with the antichrist. Through history, interpreters have identified a wide range of figures with the antichrist.

Apocalypse: From a Greek word (*apokalyptō*) that means "to reveal." Apocalypse can be used two ways: (1) It can refer to a cataclysmic event that interrupts history, ending one era and launching—revealing—another, often in a violent way. (2) It can refer to a type of literature that depicts apocalyptic events, often by using colorful images that are difficult for today's readers to understand until they are explained historically and literarily.

Apocalyptic eschatology: A form of eschatology that sees history divided into two ages (the present evil age and the coming new age, the Realm of God). God ends the present and fully and finally establishes God's rule.

Chiliasm: From the Greek word for one thousand (*chilioi*), chiliasm is another term used to speak about the millennium (Rev. 20:4–6). Often the term is used as a synonym for premillennialism, especially in its earliest forms.

Consummation: Often used as a designation for when God will end the present and will fully and finally bring God's redemptive purposes into being. Sometimes it refers to the time after the second coming of Christ, when God ends evil and puts the new world in place. This is an approximate synonym for "end times" and "last things."

Dispensationalism: The idea that God has divided history into specific eras (dispensations). Each dispensation has a particular character, e.g., law, grace. Christians have generated several different patterns of dispensations. One of the most popular today is dispensational premillennialism (*see* Premillennialism).

Divinization: See *Theosis.*

165

End Time(s): A way of speaking about the end of the present age of history and the events that accompany the second coming of Jesus; an approximate synonym for "last things" and "consummation."

Eschatology: From two Greek words: "last" (*eschatos*) and "thinking about" (*logos*). Eschatology is thinking about or formulating what one believes about the last things, that is, God's ultimate purposes for human beings and the cosmos. There are many different kinds of eschatologies. Three examples that occur frequently in this book are apocalyptic eschatology, realized eschatology, and *theosis.*

Future Eschatology: The belief that God's eschatological purposes will be fulfilled in the future.

Gnosticism: A religious movement in the ancient world, slightly later than the New Testament, that believed that the present physical world, including the body, is evil and that the nonphysical spiritual dimension of existence is good. As long as a person is alive, the nonphysical, spiritual soul is trapped in the evil body, but at death the soul can be liberated from the body and join other liberated souls in heaven. To be liberated, the person must receive secret knowledge communicated through a rite of initiation. The name "Gnosticism" comes from the Greek word *gnosis,* which is translated as "knowledge."

God's Ultimate Purpose(s): A phrase we use for what God intends for the ultimate, final destiny of individuals, communities, nature, the cosmos, and the heavenly world. These include love, justice, peace, and abundance. An approximate synonym for "eschatology."

Kingdom of God: *See* Realm of God.

Last Things: A way of speaking about the second coming of Jesus and the things that accompany it; an approximate synonym for "end times" and "consummation."

Millenarianism: The belief that society will be transformed through the assistance of supernatural action.

Millennium: From the Latin *mille,* which means "a thousand." The designation is a name for the reign of Christ and the faithful martyrs in the world for a thousand years in Revelation 20:4–6 before the final judgment and the coming of the new heaven and the new earth. Interpreters debate whether the millennium is a literary figure in the book of Revelation or is a reference to an actual historical event.

New Heaven and New Earth: A phrase from 2 Peter 3:13 and Revelation 21:1 that refers to existence after the second coming, when God fully enacts God's ultimate purposes in a new (or renewed) cosmos.

Parousia: From two Greek words meaning "being alongside" or "presence." In the New Testament, it usually refers to the second coming of Jesus: he comes from heaven to be present on the earth and do the work of an apocalyptic redeemer. *See* Second Coming.

Postmillennialism: A particular form of millennialism that assumes Christ will return after human activity brings about a period of peace and prosperity. The time frame is often understood in nonliteral terms.

Premillennialism: The belief that Christ's return will inaugurate the millennial reign of Christ on earth. It may or may not include a time of tribulation before Christ's return.

Present-Future Eschatology: God's ultimate purposes are already partially present in the world (now) but will be finally and fully in place only in the future (not yet). People and the world can experience some of God's ultimate purposes now but can wholly experience them only in the future.

Rapture: Often (but not exclusively) associated with premillennialism. It suggests that God will remove the faithful from the earth before the time of tribulation begins, so that they will not suffer along with the rest of humanity. *See* Tribulation.

Realized Eschatology: The belief that God's ultimate purposes are already present in the world. People and the world can experience those purposes now.

Realm of God: Sometimes called the Kingdom of God or the Reign of God, Dominion of God, New Age, New Creation, and similar expressions. The phrase "kingdom of heaven" is a synonym. In apocalyptic eschatology, the Realm of God is the time, activity, and place wherein God shapes everything according to God's purposes of love, justice, peace, and abundance, in contrast to the present world, which is a place of much animosity, injustice, violence, and scarcity. The present is named by such expressions as the realm of this world, the old age, the old creation, and simply "this world." In a good bit of Christian theology, the Realm is partially realized in the present and will be fully realized after the return of Jesus. In some Christian theology, the Realm is altogether future.

Reincarnation: The belief that when a human being dies, the person's soul is reborn in another person or life form. Reincarnation is not a Jewish or Christian concept.

Second Coming (Parousia): The first coming is understood to be Jesus' earthly life in the first century CE. After the resurrection, according to New Testament traditions, Jesus ascended to heaven, from which he will return to the world a second time to install the Realm of God. *See* Parousia.

Son of Man: A technical term, found in Daniel 7:13–14, for a heavenly figure whom God appoints to establish God's dominion on earth. Writers in the New Testament often apply this term to Jesus.

Theosis: A word derived from the Greek word for "God" (*theos*) and used in the Orthodox tradition for the process of salvation whereby a human being becomes ever more like God. The person does not become God but is granted union with God. This process is also known as divinization.

Tribulation: A term especially (but not exclusively) characteristic of premillennialism; a period of severe suffering in the world that precedes the return of Jesus to establish the millennium. *See* Premillennialism.

Notes

Introduction

1. For Bob's theological journey, see Robert D. Cornwall, *Called to Bless: Finding Hope by Reclaiming Our Spiritual Roots* (Eugene, OR: Cascade Books, 2021).

Chapter 1: The Old Testament

1. These documents (and many others like them) can easily be found in a collection such as James H. Charlesworth, ed., *The Old Testament Pseudepigrapha: Apocalyptic Literature and Testaments* (Garden City, NY: Doubleday, 1983), vol. 1.

Chapter 2: The New Testament

1. N. T. Wright, *Surprised by Hope: Rethinking Heaven, the Resurrection, and the Mission of the Church* (New York: HarperOne, 2008). Cf. J. Richard Middleton, *A New Heaven and a New Earth: Reclaiming Biblical Eschatology* (Grand Rapids: Baker Academic, 2014).

2. Additional key references to the second coming in Mark include Mark 8:39; 9:1; 14:62.

3. Philo's writings are available in *Philo in Ten Volumes and Two Supplementary Volumes*, ed. F. H. Coalson, J. W. Earp, Ralph Marcus, and F. H. Whitaker, The Loeb Classical Library (Cambridge: Harvard University Press, 1929–1962).

4. Philo, "On the Giants," in *Philo in Ten Volumes and Two Supplementary Volumes*, vol. 2, paragraph 14, p. 453.

Chapter 3: The Eastern Christian Church

1. Brian E. Daley, *The Hope of the Early Church: A Handbook of Patristic Eschatology* (Grand Rapids: Baker Academic, 2010), 48.

2. Clement of Alexandria, quoted in Hilarion Alfeyev, *Christ the Conqueror of Hell: The Descent into Hades from an Orthodox Perspective* (Crestwood, NY: St. Vladimir's Seminary Press, 2009), 47.

3. Origen, quoted in Alfeyev, *Christ the Conqueror of Hell*, 51.

4. Diadochus of Photiki, "Spiritual Knowledge," in Diokleia Kallistos, *The Philokalia* (Boston: Faber and Faber, 1979/1995), Kindle loc. 3755.

5. Gregory J. Riley, *The River of God: A New History of Christian Origins* (San Francisco: HarperSanFrancisco, 2003), 132.

6. Gregory of Nyssa, *On the Soul and the Resurrection*, trans. Catherine P. Roth (Crestwood, NY: St. Vladimir's Seminary Press, 1993), 84.

7. Gregory, *On the Soul*, 118.

8. Gregory, *On the Soul*, 121.

9. Gregory of Nyssa, *Catechetical Discourse: A Handbook for Catechists*, trans. Ignatius Green (Crestwood, NY: St. Vladimir's Seminary Press, 2019), 143–44.

10. Daley, *The Hope of the Early Church*, 202.

11. Maximus the Confessor, quoted in Kallistos Ware, *The Philokalia*, Kindle loc. 7831.

12. Maximus the Confessor, "Letter 14 (634–640 CE)," in Stephen J. Shoemaker, *A Prophet Has Appeared: The Rise of Islam through Christian and Jewish Eyes: A Sourcebook* (Oakland: University of California Press, 2021), 58.

13. Stephen J. Shoemaker, *The Death of a Prophet: The End of Muhammad's Life and the Beginnings of Islam* (Philadelphia: University of Pennsylvania Press, 2012), 119.

14. Saïd Amir Arjomand, "Islamic Apocalypticism in the Classic Period," in *The Continuum History of Apocalypticism*, ed. Bernard J. McGinn, John J. Collins, and Stephen J. Stein (New York: Continuum International Publishing Group, 2003), 386.

15. Seyyed Hossein Nasr, *The Study Quran: A New Translation and Commentary* (San Francisco: HarperOne, 2015).

16. "Apocalypse of Ps. Methodius," quoted in "Ps.-Methodius: A Concept of History in Response to the Rise of Islam," in G. J. Reinink, *Syriac Christianity under Late Sasanian, and Early Islamic Rule*, Variorum Collected Studies Series (Burlington, VT: Ashgate Publishing Co., 2005), IX: 169–70.

17. J. Eugene Clay, "Apocalypticism in Eastern Europe," in *The Continuum History of Apocalypticism*, 628–30.

18. Andrew Louth, *Introducing Eastern Orthodox Theology* (Downers Grove, IL: InterVarsity, 2013), intro., Kindle.

Chapter 4: Views of the Second Coming in the Christian West

1. Hippolytus, *On Christ and Antichrist*, trans. J. H. MacMahon, in *Ante-Nicene Fathers* 5, ed. Alexander Roberts, James Donaldson, and A. Cleveland Coxe (Buffalo, NY: Christian Literature Publishing Co., 1886). Revised and edited for New Advent by Kevin Knight. http://www.newadvent.org/fathers/0516.htm. See Bernard McGinn, *Visions of the End: Apocalyptic Traditions in the Middle Ages* (New York: Columbia University Press, 1998), 22.

2. Brian E. Daley, *The Hope of the Early Church: A Handbook of Patristic Eschatology* (Grand Rapids: Baker Academic, 2010), 34.

3. Daley, *Hope of the Early Church*, 130–31.

4. Daley, *Hope of the Early Church*, 132.

5. Augustine, *The City of God by Saint Augustine,* introduction by Thomas Merton, trans. Marcus Dods (New York: Modern Library, 1950), 20:7.

6. Augustine, *City of God,* 20:8.

7. Augustine, *City of God,* 22:15–16.

8. Joachim of Fiore, in *Apocalyptic Spirituality: Treatises and Letters of Lactantius, Adso of Montier-En-Der, Joachim of Fiore, The Spiritual Franciscans, Savonarola,* trans. Bernard McGinn, Classics of Western Spirituality (Mahwah, NJ: Paulist Press, 1979), 136.

Chapter 5: Views of the Second Coming in the Reformation and Beyond

1. Martin Luther, "Preface to the Revelation of Saint John (II)," in *Works of Martin Luther with Introductions and Notes: The Philadelphia Edition* (Grand Rapids: Baker Book House, 1982), 6:489.

2. Amy Frykholm, *Christian Understandings of the Future* (Minneapolis: Fortress, 2016), 235–36, Kindle.

3. Frederick J. Baumgartner, *Longing for the End: A History of Millennialism in Western Civilization* (New York: St. Martin's, 1999), 95.

4. Baumgartner, *Longing for the End*, 105.

Section Three: "Are We Going to Be 'Left Behind'?"

1. Paul Boyer, *When Time Shall Be No More: Prophecy Belief in Modern American Culture* (Cambridge, MA: The Belknap Press of Harvard University Press, 1992), 8–82. See also Martyn Whittock, *The End Times, Again? 2,000 Years of the Use and Misuse of Biblical Prophecy* (Eugene, OR: Cascade Books, 2021), 149–51.

2. Boyer, *When Time Shall Be No More*, 87.

3. Boyer, *When Time Shall Be No More*, 88.

4. Whittock, *The End Times, Again?*, 149.

Chapter 6: Premillennialism

1. Craig Blaising, "Premillennialism," in *Three Views on the Millennium and Beyond,* Counterpoints: Bible and Theology (Grand Rapids: Zondervan Academic, 1998), 162, Kindle.

Chapter 7: Postmillennialism

1. Kenneth L. Gentry Jr., "Postmillennialism," in *Three Views on the Millennium and Beyond* (Grand Rapids: Zondervan Academic, 1998), 13–14, Kindle.

2. Gustavo Gutiérrez, *A Theology of Liberation: History, Politics and Salvation,* ed. and trans. Sister Caridad Inda and John Eagleson (Maryknoll, NY: Orbis Books, 1973), 177.

3. R. J. Rushdoony, *The Institutes of Biblical Law* (Nutley, NJ: Progressive and Reformed Press, 1973), 3–4.

Section Four: "How Do We Make Sense of the Second Coming Today?"

1. See Debra Mumford, *Envisioning the Reign of God: Preaching for Tomorrow* (Valley Forge, PA: Judson, 2019), which outlines twelve ways of envisioning the reign of God.

Chapter 9: Separating the Core from the Container

1. Rudolf Bultmann, "New Testament and Mythology," in *Kerygma and Myth: A Theological Debate,* ed. H. W. Bartsch (New York: Harper & Row, 1953), 3.

Chapter 10: The Presence of the Future

1. Ernst Käsemann, *On Being a Disciple of the Crucified Nazarene: Unpublished Lectures and Sermons,* ed. Rudolf Landau and Wolfgang Kraus, trans. Roy A. Harrisville (Grand Rapids: Eerdmans, 2010), 7.

2. Jürgen Moltmann, Nicholas Wolterstorff, and Ellen T. Charry, *A Passion for God's Reign: Theology, Christian Learning, and the Christian Self,* ed. Miroslav Volf (Grand Rapids: Eerdmans, 1998), 7.

3. Jürgen Moltmann, *In the End—The Beginning: The Life of Hope,* trans. Margaret Kohl (Minneapolis: Fortress, 2004), 87–88.

4. Jürgen Moltmann, *The Coming of God: Christian Eschatology,* trans. Margaret Kohl (Minneapolis: Fortress Press, 1996), Kindle loc. 473–74.

5. Moltmann, *Passion for God's Reign,* 21.

6. Richard Bauckham, "Jürgen Moltmann," in *The Blackwell Encyclopedia of Modern Christian Thought,* ed. Alister E. McGrath (Oxford, UK: Basil Blackwell, 1993), 386.

7. Jürgen Moltmann, *Sun of Righteousness, Arise! God's Future for Humanity and the Earth,* trans. Margaret Kohl (Minneapolis: Fortress, 2010), 77.

8. Moltmann, *Sun of Righteousness,* 137.

9. Moltmann, *Sun of Righteousness,* 141.

10. Moltmann, *Sun of Righteousness,* 142.

11. Moltmann, *In the End—the Beginning,* 91.

12. Moltmann, *In the End—the Beginning,* 92.

13. Jürgen Moltmann, *Resurrected to Eternal Life, On Dying and Rising,* trans. Ellen Yutzy Glebe (Minneapolis: Fortress, 2019), 26.

Chapter 11: Creating a Just World Now and in the Future

1. Miguel A. De La Torre, *Liberation Theology for Armchair Theologians* (Louisville, KY: Westminster John Knox, 2013), 45.

2. Gustavo Gutiérrez, *A Theology of Liberation: History, Politics and Salvation,* trans. and ed. Sister Caridad Inda and John Eagleson (Maryknoll, NY: Orbis Books, 1973), 213.

3. Jon Sobrino, *Jesus the Liberator: A Historical-Theological Reading of Jesus of Nazareth,* trans. Paul Burns and Francis McDonagh (Maryknoll, NY: Orbis Books, 1993), 129.

4. José Míguez Bonino, *Doing Theology in a Revolutionary Situation* (Philadelphia: Fortress, 1975), 142.

5. James H. Cone, *God of the Oppressed,* rev. ed. (Maryknoll, NY: Orbis Books, 1997), 116.

6. Cone, *God of the Oppressed,* 118–19.

7. Míguez Bonino, *Doing Theology in a Revolutionary Situation,* 152.

Chapter 12: Open-Ended Futures

1. Thomas Jay Oord, *Open and Relational Theology: An Introduction to Life-Changing Ideas* (Nampa, ID: SacraSage Press, 2021), 113.

Chapter 13: Contemporary Eastern Orthodoxy and the Second Coming

1. Andrew Louth, *Introducing Eastern Orthodox Theology* (Downers Grove, IL: InterVarsity, 2013), chap. 9, Kindle.

2. Alexander Schmemann, *The Eucharist: Sacrament of the Kingdom*, trans. Paul Kachur (Crestwood, NY: St. Vladimir's Seminary Press, 1987), 40–41.

3. Schmemann, *Eucharist*, 48.

4. Vladimir Lossky, *Dogmatic Theology: Creation, God's Image in Man, and the Redeeming Work of the Trinity* (Crestwood, NY: St. Vladimir's Seminary Press, 2017), 162.

5. Sergius Bulgakov, *The Sophiology of Death: Essays on Eschatology: Personal, Political, Universal*, trans. Roberto J. De La Noval (Eugene, OR: Cascade Books, 2021), 90–91.

6. Vladimir Lossky, *The Mystical Theology of the Eastern Church* (Crestwood, NY: St. Vladimir's Seminary Press, 1976), 73.

7. Lossky, *The Mystical Theology of the Eastern Church*, 196–97.

8. Lossky, *Dogmatic Theology*, 161–62.

9. Lossky, *The Mystical Theology of the Eastern Church*, 197–98.

10. David Bentley Hart, *That All Shall Be Saved: Heaven, Hell, and Universal Salvation* (New Haven, CT: Yale University Press, 2019), Kindle loc. 2738.

Chapter 17: Soul and Body Separated at Death but Reunited and Transformed in Heaven

1. Augustine, *On Christian Belief*, trans. Michael O'Connell (Hyde Park, NY: New City Press, 2005), 324.

Chapter 18: The Spiritual Journey toward Union with God

1. Andrew Louth, *Introducing Eastern Orthodox Theology* (Downers Grove, IL: InterVarsity, 2013), chap. 9, Kindle.

2. Norman Russell, *Fellow Workers with God: Orthodox Thinking on Theosis* (Crestwood, NY: St. Vladimir's Seminary Press, 2009), 21.

3. Louth, *Introducing Eastern Orthodox Theology*, chap. 9.

For Further Reading

Many writers address the specific subject of the second coming of Jesus, as well as the broader topic of eschatology. We list and annotate a few reader-friendly works that go deeper and wider than the present book. We try to recommend a spread of books that consider (and sometimes evaluate) various approaches.

Bell, Rob. *Love Wins: A Book about Heaven, Hell, and the Fate of Every Person Who Ever Lived.* San Francisco, CA: HarperOne, 2011. A book at the popular level that contends God's ultimate purpose is universal salvation.

Blomberg, Craig L., and Sung Wook Chung, eds. *A Case for Historic Premillennialism: An Alternative to the "Left Behind" Eschatology.* Grand Rapids: Baker Academic, 2009. The contributors, all committed to historic premillennialism, offer reasons for holding to that position while critiquing the recent *Left Behind* mind-set.

Blaising, Craig A., Kenneth L. Gentry Jr., and Robert B. Strimple. *Three Views on the Millennium and Beyond.* Counterpoints: Bible and Theology. Grand Rapids: Zondervan Academic, 1998. Three contributors converse about the three primary millennial perspectives—premillennialism, postmillennialism, and amillennialism.

Clouse, Robert G., ed. *The Meaning of the Millennium: Four Views.* With contributions by George Eldon Ladd, Herman A. Hoyt, Loraine Boettner, and Anthony A. Hoekema. Downers Grove, IL: InterVarsity, 1970. Conversation among four viewpoints on the millennium: historic premillennialism, premillennialism, postmillennialism, and amillennialism.

Frykholm, Amy. *Christian Understandings of the Future: The Historical Trajectory.* Minneapolis: Fortress, 2016. Like the current volume, follows different interpretations of God's purposes for the future but does so in greater breadth and detail.

McDowell, John C., and Scott A. Kirkland. *Eschatology.* Guides to Theology. Grand Rapids: Eerdmans, 2018. Explains four different approaches to God's ultimate purposes: apocalyptic, existential, political, and christological.

Middleton, J. Richard. *A New Heaven and a New Earth: Reclaiming Biblical Eschatology*. Grand Rapids: Baker Academic, 2014. Interprets the Bible as presenting God's ultimate purpose as creating a new heaven and a new earth, that is, a cosmic renewal, a "holistic eschatology" that results in a certain way of life.

Mumford, Debra. *Envisioning the Reign of God: Preaching for Tomorrow*. Valley Forge, PA: Judson, 2019. Designed for preachers, this volume explains twelve different ways Christians imagine the Realm of God, including perspectives of African Americans, feminists, womanists, Latinos and Latinas, the LGBTQIA+ community, and others.

Rossing, Barbara. *The Rapture Exposed: The Message of Hope in the Book of Revelation*. New York: Basic Books, 2004. While focusing on the book of Revelation, the author criticizes premillennialism (as symbolized by the doctrine of the rapture) more widely and posits that the book of Revelation (and, in her view, good theology) is anti-rapture and affirms a renewed world.

Schwarz, Hans. *Eschatology*. Grand Rapids: Eerdmans, 2000. A wide-ranging survey of the emergence of eschatological expectation in the biblical world and "the manifold faces of eschatology," ranging from the Bible and Christian theologies through philosophy, ecology, and prospects for the future of humankind and the planet.

Whittock, Martyn. *The End Times, Again? 2,000 Years of the Use and Misuse of Biblical Prophecy*. Eugene, OR: Cascade Books, 2021. Easy to follow historical overview of the emergence of end-time speculation and how it has developed over the centuries.

Wright, N. T. *Surprised by Hope: Rethinking Heaven, the Resurrection, and the Mission of the Church*. San Francisco: HarperOne, 2008. Readable exposition of the idea that God's ultimate purpose results in a "new heaven and a new earth," that is, a renewed domain of existence.

Scripture Index

Printed in the USA
CPSIA information can be obtained
at www.ICGtesting.com
LVHW091546190424
777187LV00013B/16